TABLE OF CONTENT

Chapter 1: Introduction to Upcy

- What is upcycling? ....

- Benefits of upcycling and repu..

- Tools and materials needed 13

- Safety precautions 17

Chapter 2: Upcycling Plastic Shower Curtains 21

- Creating a waterproof tablecloth 21

- Making a shower curtain tote bag 24

- DIY plastic shower curtain liner 28

Chapter 3: Repurposing Plastic Laundry Detergent Bottles 32

- Creating a storage container for laundry supplies 32

- Making a scoop or funnel 35

- DIY planter from detergent bottles 38

Chapter 4: Repurposing Plastic Shampoo Bottles 43

- Creating a toothbrush holder 43

- DIY phone dock from shampoo bottles 46

- Plastic bottle flower vase 50

Chapter 5: Upcycling Plastic Lotion Bottles 54

- DIY storage container for small items 54

- Creating a soap dispenser 57

- Lotion bottle herb garden 60

Chapter 6: Repurposing Paper Towel Rolls 64

- Creating cord organizers 64

- Making seedling pots 67

- Paper towel roll wall art 70

Chapter 7: Upcycling Toilet Paper Rolls 75

- DIY drawer organizers 75

- Crafting mini gift boxes 78

- Toilet paper roll bird feeder 81

Chapter 8: Repurposing Plastic Grocery Bags 85

- Creating woven mats or rugs..85

- Plastic bag organizers 88

- DIY raincoat or poncho 91

Chapter 9: Repurposing Plastic Food Packaging...............95

- Creating mini storage containers......................................95

- Making a DIY wallet 99

- Plastic packaging planters 103

Chapter 10: Upcycling Plastic Clamshell Containers 107

- Creating a travel jewelry case..107

- DIY succulent planter..110

- Plastic clamshell organizer...115

Chapter 11: Repurposing Plastic Takeout Containers......119

- Lunchbox from takeout containers 119

- DIY planters for herbs or flowers...................................122

- Takeout container drawer dividers 124

Chapter 12: Upcycling Plastic Egg Cartons.....................128

- Creating a seed starter tray 128

- DIY Christmas ornaments..................131
- Egg carton jewelry organizer 135

Chapter 13: Repurposing Plastic Milk Jugs.................139
- Plastic milk jug watering can.........................139
- DIY bird feeder 142
- Milk jug herb garden.............................144

Chapter 14: Upcycling Plastic Soda Bottles 148
- Crafting a piggy bank 148
- DIY vertical garden 152
- Plastic bottle broom..............................155

Chapter 15: Repurposing Wine Corks 159
- Creating a corkboard 159
- Wine cork keychain or necklace 161
- DIY stamp for crafts 164

Chapter 16: Upcycling Wine Bottles 168
- Making a decorative candle holder..............168
- Wine bottle chandelier 171
- DIY vase from wine bottles.........................175

Chapter 17: Repurposing Glass Jars 181
- Creating storage containers 181
- Crafting a homemade snow globe..............184
- Glass jar lanterns..............................187

Chapter 18: Upcycling Glass Bottles 191
- DIY bottle lamps..............................191
- Creating a bottle vase or centerpiece...........194

- *Glass bottle wind chimes*..198

Chapter 19: Repurposing Tin Cans......................................203

- *Tin can planters*...203

- *DIY tin can lanterns*..206

- *Tin can pencil holder*..210

Chapter 20: Upcycling Aluminum Cans................................213

- *Creating a soda can herb garden*.................................213

- *DIY aluminum can coasters*..216

- *Aluminum can flower ornaments*.................................219

Chapter 21: Repurposing Paper Bags..................................223

- *Creating gift wrap or gift bags*....................................223

- *DIY paper bag lanterns*..226

- *Paper bag scrapbook album*..230

Chapter 1: Introduction to Upcycling and Repurposing

- What is upcycling?

Upcycling and repurposing have gained tremendous popularity in recent years for their ability to transform everyday items into functional and stylish creations. This innovative DIY practice puts sustainability and creativity at the forefront, allowing us to find new and exciting uses for materials that would otherwise end up in the trash. In this chapter, we will explore the concept of upcycling and repurposing, focusing on its definition and the benefits it offers.

Upcycling can be best described as the process of taking an item that has reached the end of its original purpose and giving it new life by turning it into something of higher value or usefulness. Unlike recycling, which involves breaking down materials into their component parts and then reusing them to create something entirely new, upcycling preserves the original form and characteristics of the item, adding value through creative additions or transformations.

The main goal of upcycling is to reduce waste and minimize our environmental impact by finding alternative uses for materials, prolonging their lifespan, and avoiding their disposal into landfills or incinerators. By upcycling, we can help conserve natural resources, reduce energy consumption, and decrease the emission of greenhouse gases associated with the production of new materials.

Now, let's delve into the intriguing world of upcycling and repurposing, where we will uncover creative ways to reuse common household items and give them a whole new purpose. In this guide, we will explore various materials commonly found in our homes and discuss fascinating DIY projects that will transform them into functional and stylish creations.

Plastic Shower Curtains.

Plastic shower curtains are often replaced when they become worn or no longer suit our bathroom decor. Instead of throwing them away, consider upcycling them into functional and stylish items. One idea is to use the shower curtain as a protective covering for outdoor furniture. By cutting the shower curtain to size, you can create custom-fit covers that keep your furniture safe from the elements. Another creative use for plastic shower curtains is to transform them into waterproof tote bags. By sewing the curtains together and adding sturdy handles, you can create versatile bags that are perfect for trips to the beach or grocery shopping during rainy days.

Plastic Laundry Detergent Bottles.

Empty plastic laundry detergent bottles can be given a new lease on life through upcycling. One unique idea is to transform them into storage containers. Simply cut the top section of the bottle, leaving a sturdy base and a wide opening. Then, use colorful adhesive paper or paint to decorate the container and personalize it to your liking. This repurposed container can be used to store a variety of small items, such as craft supplies, office stationery, or even kitchen utensils. By repurposing laundry detergent bottles, not only do we save money on buying new containers, but we also reduce our plastic waste footprint.

Plastic Shampoo Bottles.

Similar to plastic laundry detergent bottles, plastic shampoo bottles can be repurposed into practical storage solutions. One popular idea is to turn them into hanging organizers for the bathroom or kitchen. By cutting off the top section of the bottle, leaving the handle intact, we can create a storage pocket. Attach the bottles to the wall using adhesive hooks or screws, and use them to store items like toothbrushes, toothpaste, or kitchen utensils. This not only declutters your space but also adds a unique touch of creativity to your home decor.

Plastic Lotion Bottles.

Plastic lotion bottles can be upcycled into charming decorative items for your outdoor spaces. By cutting off the top section of the bottle and cleaning it thoroughly, you can create small planters for herbs or flowers. Paint the bottles with vibrant colors or patterns, and add drainage holes at the bottom for proper water flow. These repurposed planters can then be hung from a tree branch or displayed on a balcony railing, instantly adding a touch of greenery and beauty to your outdoor living spaces.

By repurposing everyday items like shower curtains, laundry detergent bottles, shampoo bottles, and lotion bottles, we are not only reducing waste but also tapping into our creativity to create unique and functional pieces for our homes. Stay tuned for the next chapter, where we will explore more fascinating DIY ideas for repurposing and upcycling common household materials.

- Benefits of upcycling and repurposing

Dive into the world of upcycling and repurposing! In this chapter, we will explore the benefits of transforming everyday items into functional and stylish creations. Through this guide, we hope to inspire you to look at discarded materials in a new light and discover the endless possibilities they hold. So, without further ado, let's delve into the exciting realm of upcycling and repurposing!.

One of the most compelling reasons to engage in upcycling and repurposing is the positive impact it has on the environment. By upcycling and repurposing materials, you are diverting waste from landfills and reducing the demand for new production. This, in turn, helps in conserving natural resources, minimizing pollution, and decreasing energy consumption. Whether it's transforming plastic shower curtains, laundry detergent bottles, shampoo bottles, or lotion bottles, each repurposed item contributes to a greener planet.

Moreover, upcycling and repurposing offer countless opportunities for creativity and self-expression. Creating something new and unique out of seemingly ordinary materials allows you to showcase your individuality and crafting skills. It gives you the chance to put your personal touch on everyday items and turn them into functional works of art. Whether it's turning paper towel rolls or toilet paper rolls into creative storage solutions or transforming plastic grocery bags into fashionable tote bags, the possibilities for creative expression are limitless.

Another notable benefit of upcycling and repurposing is the sense of satisfaction and accomplishment it brings. Completing a DIY project using repurposed materials gives you a sense of pride in your resourcefulness and ingenuity. It allows you to tap into your problem-solving abilities and challenges you to think outside the box. The satisfaction of breathing new life into something that would otherwise be discarded is truly rewarding.

Furthermore, upcycling and repurposing can save you money. Instead of buying new items, repurposing materials allows you to create functional and stylish alternatives cost-effectively. With a little bit of imagination and some basic tools, you can transform plastic clamshell containers, takeout containers, or egg cartons into decorative storage solutions or even unique planters. By upcycling, you not only save money but also have the opportunity to customize items to suit your specific needs and tastes.

Lastly, upcycling and repurposing support sustainable living. In a society characterized by fast fashion and disposable products, choosing to repurpose and upcycle demonstrates a conscious effort to reduce waste and promote longevity. By upcycling and repurposing, you are extending the lifespan of materials and embracing a more sustainable lifestyle. Whether it's repurposing plastic milk jugs or soda bottles into innovative household decor or turning wine corks, wine bottles, glass jars, or glass bottles into eye-catching DIY projects, each repurposed item serves as a tangible reminder of sustainable living.

They contribute to the protection of the environment, offer opportunities for creativity, provide a sense of satisfaction, save money, and support sustainable living. Through this chapter, we have just scratched the surface of the vast and exciting world of upcycling and repurposing. So grab your tools, let your imagination run wild, and embark on a journey of transforming everyday items into extraordinary creations!.

- Tools and materials needed

In order to upcycle and repurpose various everyday items, such as plastic shower curtains, laundry detergent bottles, shampoo bottles, lotion bottles, paper towel rolls, toilet paper rolls, plastic grocery bags, food packaging, clamshell containers, takeout containers, egg cartons, milk jugs, soda bottles, wine corks, wine bottles, glass jars, glass bottles, tin cans, aluminum cans, and paper bags, you will need a range of tools and materials to successfully transform them into functional and stylish creations.

To get started, it's important to have a good set of basic tools in your DIY arsenal. Some essential tools that will come in handy for upcycling and repurposing projects include a pair of sharp scissors, a utility knife, a hot glue gun with glue sticks, a ruler or measuring tape, a hole punch, a set of screwdrivers in various sizes, needle-nose pliers, wire cutters, a staple gun, and a heat gun or hairdryer for shaping and bending materials. These tools will help you to cut, shape, adhere, and manipulate the everyday items you plan to upcycle and repurpose.

Additionally, there are certain materials that are helpful when working with specific items. For plastic shower curtains, laundry detergent bottles, shampoo bottles, lotion bottles, and other plastic containers, you may need adhesive stickers or decals, acrylic paint, spray paint, or waterproof outdoor paint, as well as decorative elements such as ribbon, buttons, or beads to add a touch of style. Depending on the project, you may also need sandpaper or a file to smooth any rough edges.

When working with paper towel rolls, toilet paper rolls, and plastic grocery bags, you can benefit from having craft paper, wrapping paper, or fabric to cover and decorate these items. Adhesive tape, glue, or Mod Podge can also be helpful to secure materials and add extra durability. Embellishments like washi tape, feathers, or fabric scraps can be used for additional decoration.

For plastic food packaging, such as clamshell containers and takeout containers, you might consider using ribbons, decorative paper, or fabric to transform them into attractive storage or display solutions. Adhesive labels for organization and clear sealant spray to protect your creations are also useful materials to have on hand.

When repurposing plastic egg cartons, milk jugs, soda bottles, and other plastic containers, you may require a craft knife or scissors for cutting, as well as acrylic paint, spray paint, or markers to personalize them. Other elements like googly eyes, pipe cleaners, or construction paper can be used to turn these items into fun and whimsical crafts.

Wine corks, wine bottles, glass jars, and glass bottles offer a wide range of upcycling possibilities. To work with these materials, you will need a glass cutter, sandpaper, or a file for shaping and smoothing edges. Various paints, including glass paints and chalk paints, can be used to create unique designs. Additionally, candle-making supplies, such as wicks and wax, can transform glass containers into beautiful homemade candles.

When repurposing tin cans and aluminum cans, you should have a can opener, pliers, gloves, or other protective gear to prevent injuries while working with sharp edges. Sanders or sandpaper can help you create a smooth surface for painting or decorating. Paint or decorative paper can then be applied to customize these items, turning them into functional storage or decorative pieces.

As for paper bags, you can use them as a base for various projects. You will need crafting punches, stamps, or stencils to create intricate designs. Fabric or ribbons can be added as handles or decorative elements. Acrylic paint, spray paint, or markers can be used to bring color and flair to your creations.

By having the right tools and materials, you can successfully upcycle and repurpose these everyday items into functional and stylish creations. Let your creativity flow as you transform these ordinary objects into extraordinary pieces, and enjoy the satisfaction of giving them a new lease on life.

- Safety precautions

Dive into the wonderful world of upcycling and repurposing! In this chapter, we will dive into the basics of transforming everyday items into functional and stylish creations. Before we begin, it's essential to remember that safety should always be a top priority when working on any DIY project. Let's explore the safety measures for some common items: plastic shower curtains, plastic laundry detergent bottles, plastic shampoo bottles, plastic lotion bottles, paper towel rolls, toilet paper rolls, plastic grocery bags, plastic food packaging, plastic clamshell containers, plastic takeout containers, plastic egg cartons, plastic milk jugs, plastic soda bottles, wine corks, wine bottles, glass jars, glass bottles, tin cans, aluminum cans, and paper bags.

When working with plastic shower curtains, it is crucial to ensure proper ventilation in your workspace. Some plastic shower curtains may contain harmful chemicals, such as PVC or phthalates. These chemicals can be released into the air when cutting or heating the plastic. Wear protective gloves and a mask, and work in a well-ventilated area or use a respiratory protection device, such as a particulate filter mask, to avoid inhaling any potential toxins.

Plastic laundry detergent bottles, plastic shampoo bottles, and plastic lotion bottles can also pose safety risks during upcycling. Since these bottles are often made of sturdy plastic, sharp tools may be required for cutting, shaping, or repurposing them. Always wear protective gloves and safety glasses when working with sharp objects to prevent any accidental injuries. Use caution when handling tools such as utility knives or scissors and ensure they are sharp and in good condition to minimize the risk of slips or accidents.

Paper towel rolls and toilet paper rolls are commonly used in various upcycling projects. As a precautionary measure, make sure to remove any residual paper scraps from the rolls before using them. This will reduce the risk of fire hazards and other potential safety issues during the DIY process. Additionally, keep these rolls stored in a dry place to prevent mold growth or pest infestation.

When reusing plastic grocery bags, plastic food packaging, plastic clamshell containers, and plastic takeout containers, it's important to exercise caution with heat sources. Some plastics may release harmful fumes or even melt when exposed to heat. Avoid using direct heat sources, such as open flames or hot surfaces, when upcycling these items. Opt for safer alternatives like heat guns or hairdryers set on low heat, ensuring you maintain a safe distance to prevent accidental burns or damage to the plastic.

Plastic egg cartons, plastic milk jugs, and plastic soda bottles require careful handling due to their potential sharp edges. Take extra precautions to smooth down any rough edges or remove them entirely to avoid injury when using these items in your upcycling projects. Sandpaper or a utility knife can be used to achieve smooth edges and protect yourself and others from cuts or scrapes.

Let's move on to wine corks, wine bottles, glass jars, and glass bottles. Safety becomes a primary concern when working with glass materials due to the likelihood of breakage and resulting sharp edges. Wear cut-resistant gloves when handling glass to protect your hands from any potential accidents or cuts. Take care when cutting or shaping glass materials using appropriate tools and techniques. If possible, consider using pre-cut glass pieces or seek professional assistance if you're not confident in your ability to work with glass safely.

Finally, when dealing with tin cans, aluminum cans, and paper bags, make sure to exercise caution when handling sharp edges. Always wear protective gloves and use appropriate tools to avoid injury. It's advisable to blunt or fold in any sharp edges before incorporating these materials into your upcycling projects.

Remember, it's crucial to adapt these measures to the specific materials and tools you are working with. Stay vigilant, take the necessary precautions, and enjoy the process of transforming everyday items into functional and stylish creations.

Chapter 2: Upcycling Plastic Shower Curtains

- Creating a waterproof tablecloth

This DIY project is not only practical but also environmentally-friendly, as it gives a new life to materials that would otherwise end up in landfills. So, let's delve into the detailed guide on how to transform your old plastic shower curtains into a beautiful and functional tablecloth.

Before we proceed, make sure you have gathered all the materials required for this project. Apart from the plastic shower curtains, you will also need a pair of sharp scissors or craft knife, a ruler or measuring tape, a sewing machine or strong fabric glue, and any additional embellishments or decorations you may wish to add to your tablecloth.

To start, thoroughly clean and dry your plastic shower curtains. Remove any metal grommets or hooks, as they will not be necessary for this project. Lay the shower curtains flat on a large working surface and use a ruler or measuring tape to measure the desired size of your tablecloth. Keep in mind that it should comfortably fit your table with some overhang.

Once you have measured and marked the dimensions of your tablecloth, carefully cut the plastic shower curtains using sharp scissors or a craft knife. Take your time during this step to ensure straight and even cuts. It is recommended to cut along the existing hems and top edge of the shower curtains to minimize fraying.

Next, decide whether you want a simple plain tablecloth or if you'd like to add some personal flair. If you prefer a plain tablecloth, proceed to the next step. However, if you want to add some decorative elements, this is the time to do so. You can apply fabric paint, use stencils, or even attach fabric patches to create unique patterns or designs. Let your creativity run wild!.

Moving on to assembling the tablecloth, you have two options. If you are skilled with a sewing machine, you can opt to sew the cut edges together using a sturdy thread. Remember to leave a small opening to turn the tablecloth right-side out. Once all the edges have been sewn, carefully turn the tablecloth right-side out through the opening and stitch it closed. This method will provide a neat and durable finish.

Alternatively, if you do not have access to a sewing machine or prefer a no-sew project, you can use strong fabric glue to bond the cut edges together. Apply the glue sparingly along the edges, making sure to press firmly to secure the bond. It is advisable to work in small sections to prevent the glue from drying out before you finish.

After you have completed the assembly, allow the glue or stitches to fully dry and set. Once dry, your waterproof tablecloth made from upcycled plastic shower curtains is ready to be showcased on your table. It is important to note that this tablecloth can be easily wiped clean with a damp cloth or sponge, making it ideal for outdoor picnics or family gatherings.

Remember, the possibilities for upcycling and repurposing everyday items are endless. Along with plastic shower curtains, you can explore using other materials such as plastic laundry detergent bottles, shampoo bottles, lotion bottles, paper towel rolls, toilet paper rolls, plastic grocery bags, plastic food packaging, plastic clamshell containers, plastic takeout containers, plastic egg cartons, plastic milk jugs, plastic soda bottles, wine corks, wine bottles, glass jars, glass bottles, tin cans, aluminum cans, and paper bags. Each material has its unique properties and can be transformed into something functional and stylish with a little creativity.

So, unleash your inner artisan and have fun experimenting with upcycling and repurposing materials to create unique and sustainable creations. Happy crafting!.

- Making a shower curtain tote bag

We will explore the exciting process of upcycling plastic shower curtains into a functional and stylish tote bag. By repurposing these curtains, we can contribute to a more sustainable lifestyle while also creating a unique accessory. .

To get started, gather all the materials needed for this project, including a plastic shower curtain, scissors, a sewing machine or needle and thread, fabric markers or paint (optional), and any embellishments you desire. .

The first step is to prepare the shower curtain for transformation. Lay it out on a flat surface and cut it into two equal-sized rectangles. The size will depend on how big you want your tote bag to be, so measure accordingly. .

Next, fold one of the rectangular pieces in half, placing the sides with the design or pattern facing inward. This will be the main body of your tote bag. .

Using your sewing machine or needle and thread, stitch the two sides together, leaving the upper edge open. If using a sewing machine, reinforce the stitches by backstitching at the beginning and end. Repeat this step with the other rectangular piece to create the bag's lining. .

Now that you have your bag's body and lining, it's time to attach them together. Turn the bag's body right-side out and keep the lining inside out. Insert the lining into the body, ensuring that the top edges align. .

To secure the bag and create a neat finish, pin the edges together. Seam the top edge using a sewing machine or a needle and thread. You can choose to sew a regular straight stitch or explore decorative stitches for added flair. .

Once you have completed the sewing process, turn the bag right-side out through the opening left in the lining. Push the lining inside the bag and gently press the seams to give it a crisp look. .

Now comes the fun part – personalizing your tote bag! This is where you can let your creativity shine. Consider using fabric markers or paint to add unique designs or patterns onto the fabric. You can also attach embellishments like buttons, patches, or ribbons to showcase your personal style. .

Lastly, finish off your tote bag by adding sturdy handles. You can repurpose existing materials like fabric belts, braided strips of old t-shirts, or even nylon webbing. Ensure the handles are long enough to comfortably carry the bag over your shoulder or by hand. Attach them securely to both sides of the bag, reinforcing the stitches for durability. .

Once your tote bag is complete, give it a final inspection to make sure all the seams are secure and the handles are firmly attached. Clean any loose threads or marks that may have occurred during the process. .

Congratulations! You have successfully transformed a plastic shower curtain into a functional and stylish tote bag. Now, head out and proudly carry your unique creation while spreading the message of sustainability and creativity. .

Remember, upcycling and repurposing everyday items allows us to reduce waste and give new life to materials that might otherwise end up in landfills. Each project we undertake is a step towards a more sustainable future, so let your imagination run wild and try out different upcycling ideas with various materials mentioned earlier in this book. Happy crafting!.

- DIY plastic shower curtain liner

Plastic shower curtains are readily available and can easily be transformed into a versatile liner that not only serves its purpose but also adds a unique touch to your bathroom decor. So, let's dive in and discover the step-by-step instructions for this exciting upcycling project!.

1. Plastic shower curtain: Choose a curtain that complements your bathroom color scheme and style. Ensure that it is made of durable plastic to withstand the moist environment.

Now, let's jump into the process of upcycling and repurposing:

1. Clean the curtain: Start by giving the plastic shower curtain a thorough cleaning. Remove any mold, mildew, or soap scum by wiping it down with a mild detergent and warm water. Rinse it thoroughly to remove any residue.

2. Measure and cut: Place the cleaned plastic shower curtain on a flat surface. Measure the length and width of your shower stall and use these measurements to cut the shower curtain to fit the dimensions of your shower. Use a sharp pair of scissors or a utility knife for precise cuts.

3. Reinforce the edges: To prevent the plastic curtain from unraveling, reinforce the cut edges. You can achieve this by folding over the edges and securing them with waterproof tape or stitching them using a sewing machine.

4. These can be purchased at most craft or hardware stores and come in various sizes and finishes. Follow the manufacturer's instructions to install them securely.

5. You can use fabric paint, stencils, or even fabric scraps to create patterns or designs on the curtain. This will transform it from a simple liner into a personalized statement piece for your bathroom.

6. Spray some water onto the liner, making sure to cover all areas, and observe if any water seeps through. If any leakage occurs, consider reinforcing those areas with waterproof sealant or adding an additional layer to improve its water resistance.

7. Use shower curtain hooks or rings to secure it to the curtain rod. Adjust the length if necessary, ensuring it reaches down to the floor or slightly below to provide proper coverage.

This upcycling project not only reduces waste but also allows you to create a unique and personalized bathroom accessory. Whether you're interested in adding a pop of color, incorporating a specific pattern, or simply being environmentally conscious, this DIY project is a fantastic way to achieve all these goals. Start upcycling today and transform everyday items into functional and stylish creations for your home!.

Chapter 3: Repurposing Plastic Laundry Detergent Bottles

- Creating a storage container for laundry supplies

This project is perfect for those looking to organize their laundry room in a sustainable and creative way.

To begin, gather the following materials: plastic laundry detergent bottles, scissors, marker or pen, adhesive or glue, and any additional decorative items such as paint or stickers.

Start by thoroughly cleaning and drying the plastic detergent bottles. It's important to remove any labels or adhesive residue before proceeding. Once clean, decide on the desired size for your storage container. You can either use one bottle to create a single compartment container or cut multiple bottles to create separate compartments for different laundry supplies.

Using the marker or pen, draw a line on the bottle to indicate where you want to cut. This line will serve as a guide for the next step. Carefully cut along the marked line using the scissors, ensuring a smooth and even cut. Repeat this process if you're using multiple bottles for separate compartments.

Once the bottles are cut, you can further customize the storage container by adding handles or decorative elements. If you prefer a more polished look, consider sanding the edges of the cut bottles to create a smooth finish. This step is optional, but it can enhance the overall appearance of your storage container.

Now it's time to assemble the storage container. Apply adhesive or glue along the edges of the bottles where they will connect. Press the pieces together firmly, ensuring a secure bond. Allow the adhesive or glue to fully dry before moving on to the next step.

To maximize the functionality of the storage container, you can add dividers or compartments inside each section. You can achieve this by cutting smaller pieces of plastic bottles and gluing them vertically or horizontally inside the larger compartments. These dividers will help keep smaller items, such as laundry pods or dryer sheets, organized and easily accessible.

Once the storage container is completely assembled, you can personalize it further by painting or decorating it to match your laundry room decor. Use acrylic paint or markers to add color or patterns, or apply stickers or decals for a more whimsical touch. This step is entirely up to your personal preference and creativity.

Finally, arrange your laundry supplies inside the newly created storage container. You can organize items by type or size, ensuring a neat and clutter-free laundry room. The dividers, if added, will help keep everything in its rightful place, making it easier to find and access supplies when needed.

By upcycling these everyday items, you not only declutter your laundry room but also contribute to reducing waste and fostering creativity. Give it a try and enjoy the results of your unique and functional creation.

- Making a scoop or funnel

Creating a scoop or funnel out of everyday items can be a fun and practical project that allows for upcycling and repurposing. In this guide, we will focus specifically on repurposing plastic laundry detergent bottles to make a scoop or funnel. Plastic laundry detergent bottles are a versatile material that can easily be transformed into useful tools for various purposes.

To begin, gather your plastic laundry detergent bottles, ensuring they are clean and dry. Look for bottles with a wide opening at the top so you can easily create a scoop or funnel shape. Use scissors or a craft knife to carefully cut off the bottom of the bottle. This will create an open end that will serve as the scoop or funnel.

Next, decide whether you want to create a scoop or a funnel. If you choose to make a scoop, simply round the edges of the cut end to create a smooth and curved surface. Take your time to ensure the edges are even and smooth, as this will make it easier to scoop up various materials. You can also sand the edges if desired.

If you prefer to make a funnel, leave the cut end as it is without rounding it. This will provide a wider opening for pouring and transferring liquids or other materials. It's a good idea to smooth any rough edges with sandpaper to avoid any sharp edges that may cause injury.

Once you have created your scoop or funnel shape, you can personalize it further if desired. Consider using decorative duct tape or spray paint to add a touch of color and style. You can also label the scoop or funnel using waterproof markers or adhesive labels for easy identification.

The repurposed plastic laundry detergent bottle scoop or funnel can be used in various ways. For example, it can be used in the kitchen for measuring and transferring dry ingredients such as flour, sugar, or rice. In the garden, it can be handy for scooping soil, seeds, or fertilizer. Alternatively, it can be used in the garage or workshop for pouring liquids such as oils, detergents, or paints.

Remember, the possibilities are endless when it comes to repurposing plastic laundry detergent bottles. They can serve as convenient tools, reducing waste and adding functionality to your daily activities. Get creative and experiment with different bottle sizes and shapes to create a collection of scoops and funnels for various purposes around your home.

Upcycling and repurposing everyday items allows us to transform them into functional and stylish creations while contributing to a more sustainable lifestyle. Enjoy the process of creating your own scoop or funnel using plastic laundry detergent bottles and discover the countless uses it can have in your day-to-day activities.

- DIY planter from detergent bottles

In this chapter, we will explore how to repurpose plastic laundry detergent bottles into stylish and functional DIY planters. Upcycling and repurposing everyday items allows us to reduce waste and create unique pieces that reflect our personal style. With some creativity and a few simple steps, you can transform plastic laundry detergent bottles into beautiful planters that will add life and charm to any space.

To begin, gather the following materials:

1. Plastic laundry detergent bottles: Choose bottles that are empty and clean. Remove any labels or adhesive residue, as these can interfere with the aesthetics of the final product.

2. Utility knife or sharp scissors: These tools will be essential for cutting and shaping the detergent bottles.

3. Sandpaper or abrasive sponge: Use sandpaper or an abrasive sponge to smooth out any rough edges or imperfections.

4. Acrylic paint or spray paint: Choose a paint color that complements your décor and personal taste. Acrylic paint or spray paint are ideal for this project as they adhere well to plastic surfaces.

5. Paintbrushes or spray paint nozzle: Depending on the paint you choose, you will need either brushes or a spray paint nozzle. Select brushes of various sizes to accommodate different paint strokes and designs.

6. Potting soil: This is the medium in which your plants will grow. Use a quality potting soil appropriate for indoor or outdoor use, depending on where you plan to place your DIY planter.

7. Plants or seedlings: Choose plants that are suitable for the conditions in which you will be placing your planter. Consider factors such as sunlight, humidity, and temperature.

1. Prepare the detergent bottles: Begin by thoroughly cleaning and drying the plastic laundry detergent bottles. Ensure that all traces of detergent have been removed, as you don't want any chemicals to harm your plants. Remove the bottle cap and cut out the desired shape or size for your planter. Consider factors such as the plant's root structure and the space available for proper growth.

2. Smooth rough edges: Use sandpaper or an abrasive sponge to smooth the cut edges of the bottles. This step will not only enhance the appearance of your planter but also prevent any potential injuries from sharp edges.

3. Paint the planter: Depending on the desired look, you can either use acrylic paint and brushes or

spray paint to coat the exterior of the planter. Apply several coats if needed, allowing each layer to dry completely before adding the next. Feel free to get creative with patterns, designs, or even stencils to give your planter a unique touch.

4. Allow the paint to dry: Patience is key at this stage. Ensure that the paint has fully dried before proceeding to the next step. Admire your work and imagine how it will look once filled with greenery!.

5. Add drainage holes (optional): If your plastic detergent bottles do not have drainage holes, you may consider adding a few to prevent waterlogging. Use a sharp tool such as a heated nail or a drill to create small holes at the base of the planter.

6. Fill the planter with soil: Now it's time to fill your DIY planter with potting soil. Leave enough space at the top for planting the desired flowers, herbs, or plants.

7. Plant your desired greenery: Carefully transfer your chosen plants or seedlings into the

planter. Ensure that they are well-watered and properly positioned in the soil.

8. Display and maintain your DIY planter: Find the perfect spot to display your newly created planter. Be mindful of the plant's sunlight and water requirements. Regularly water your plants to keep them healthy and thriving.

By repurposing plastic laundry detergent bottles, you have not only contributed to waste reduction but also created a one-of-a-kind planter that adds beauty to your surroundings. Experiment with different bottle shapes and colors to create a stunning collection of planters that showcase your creative prowess. Happy upcycling!.

Chapter 4: Repurposing Plastic Shampoo Bottles

- Creating a toothbrush holder

This DIY project allows you to give a new life to discarded plastic bottles and create a functional and stylish accessory for your bathroom. Let's get started!.

To begin, gather your materials. You will need:

- Plastic shampoo bottles (preferably sturdy ones).
- Scissors or a craft knife.
- Sandpaper or a sanding block.
- Acrylic paint or spray paint.
- Paintbrushes (if using acrylic paint).

- Hot glue gun and glue sticks.

- Decorative elements (such as stickers or decoupage paper).

- Optional: rope, ribbon, or any other material for embellishment.

Firstly, wash and dry the plastic shampoo bottles thoroughly to remove any residue. It's important to start with clean bottles to ensure the best results.

Next, determine the size and shape of your toothbrush holder. You can either use the whole plastic bottle or cut it to your desired height. If you choose to cut the bottle, use scissors or a craft knife to carefully remove the top part of the bottle. Smooth out any rough edges with sandpaper or a sanding block.

Once you have your desired shape, it's time to add some flair to the toothbrush holder. You can paint the bottle using acrylic paint or spray paint. Choose a color that fits your bathroom decor or opt for a bold and vibrant shade to make a statement. If using acrylic paint, apply it evenly using a paintbrush. Allow the paint to dry completely before moving on to the next step.

For added visual interest, you can also decorate the toothbrush holder with stickers or decoupage paper. Apply them to the painted surface using a thin layer of Mod Podge, and seal with another layer for protection. This step is optional but can make your toothbrush holder even more unique and visually appealing.

After decorating, attach the top and bottom parts of the bottle using a hot glue gun. Be mindful of the overall structure and stability, ensuring that the parts are securely in place before proceeding.

If desired, you can add embellishments to the toothbrush holder. Consider wrapping rope, ribbon, or any other material around the base of the holder for added texture and visual interest. This step is optional and allows you to personalize the design further.

Once everything is in place and dry, your DIY toothbrush holder is ready to be used! Simply place your toothbrushes and other oral care items inside, and enjoy the functional and visually appealing accessory you've created.

Remember, this project's focus is on repurposing plastic shampoo bottles to create a toothbrush holder. However, the book Upcycle and Repurpose provides many more inspiring ideas for reusing other everyday items such as plastic shower curtains, laundry detergent bottles, paper towel rolls, and more. We encourage you to explore those chapters for additional creative upcycling projects.

By repurposing plastic shampoo bottles into a toothbrush holder, you not only reduce waste but also showcase your DIY skills and creativity. Enjoy the process of transforming everyday items into functional and stylish creations while making a positive impact on the environment. Happy crafting!.

- DIY phone dock from shampoo bottles

In this chapter, we will explore the creative process of repurposing plastic shampoo bottles to create a DIY phone dock. With a bit of imagination and some simple tools, you can transform these everyday items into a functional and stylish creation.

Firstly, gather all the materials you will need:

- Plastic shampoo bottles.

- Scissors or a craft knife.

- Sandpaper or a sanding block.

- Washi tape or decorative paper.

- Glue or adhesive tape.

- A marker or pen.

- A ruler.

- Optional: paint or spray paint for a more personalized finish.

Now, let's dive into the step-by-step instructions for creating your very own DIY phone dock:

1. Start by cleaning and drying the plastic shampoo bottles thoroughly. Remove any labels or adhesive residues from the surface.

2. Using scissors or a craft knife, carefully cut off the top portion of the shampoo bottle. This will serve as the base of your phone dock. Make sure to leave enough space to accommodate your phone comfortably.

3. Use sandpaper or a sanding block to smooth out any rough edges or sharp corners left after cutting. This will create a clean and polished look for your phone dock.

4. Take the marker or pen and mark the spot on the base where you want to insert your phone charger. Measure the width of your charger and make a corresponding mark on opposite sides of the bottle. These marks will serve as a guide for cutting out a slit for the charger.

5. Using the scissors or craft knife, carefully cut out a straight slit between the two marked spots.

Ensure that the slit is wide enough to accommodate your phone charger without any resistance.

6. Now, it's time to add a touch of style to your DIY phone dock. You can choose to cover the exterior of the bottle with decorative paper or washi tape to give it a more personalized look. Measure and cut the paper or tape to fit the surface of the bottle, and use glue or adhesive tape to securely attach it.

7. If you prefer a more uniform and sleek appearance, you can also paint the entire surface of the bottle with acrylic paint or spray paint. Choose a color that matches your personal taste or complements your existing decor.

8. Once the paint or decorative covering is dry, your DIY phone dock is ready for use. Simply insert your phone charger into the slit, place your phone on the base, and enjoy your newly repurposed creation.

Remember, the possibilities for repurposing plastic shampoo bottles are endless. You can experiment with different designs, sizes, and colors to create a phone dock that truly reflects your style and personality. Get creative and have fun with this DIY project!.

By following these step-by-step instructions, you can transform these everyday items into a DIY phone dock that is both functional and stylish. Embrace your inner artisan and enjoy the process of creating something unique with your own hands.

- *Plastic bottle flower vase*

In this chapter, we will explore the repurposing potential of plastic shampoo bottles. These everyday items often end up in the trash, contributing to environmental waste.

1. Gather the materials:

- Plastic shampoo bottle: Choose a bottle with a shape and size that suits your preferences.

- Scissors or craft knife: Use these tools to cut the plastic bottle.

- Sandpaper or emery board: This will help smooth the edges after cutting.

- Decorative materials (optional): Ribbons, twine, fabric, paints, or any other embellishments you desire.

2. Preparing the plastic bottle:

- Start by thoroughly cleaning the shampoo bottle, ensuring it is free from any residue or labels.

- Use the scissors or craft knife to carefully cut the top off the bottle, just below the neck. You can cut straight across or create a scalloped or zigzag pattern for a decorative touch.

- If needed, use sandpaper or an emery board to smooth any rough edges from the cut.

3. Adding decorative details (optional):

You can wrap ribbons or twine around the bottle, glue on fabric or paper cutouts, or apply paint to achieve the desired look. Let your imagination run wild!.

4. Preparing the vase for flowers:

- Fill the bottom of your plastic bottle vase with a small amount of water. This will provide a stable base for your flowers and help them stay fresh for longer.

- Arrange your chosen blooms in the vase, trimming the stems to the desired length.

5. Maintenance and care:

- If the vase becomes stained or discolored over time, consider painting it or covering it with decorative materials to give it a fresh new look.

- Additionally, be mindful of where you place your vase, as prolonged exposure to direct sunlight can cause the plastic to degrade over time.

By following these instructions and repurposing plastic shampoo bottles into flower vases, you not only contribute to reducing waste but also add a unique and eco-friendly touch to your home decor.

Remember, this is just one of the many creative ways to upcycle and repurpose everyday items. " Happy crafting!.

Chapter 5: Upcycling Plastic Lotion Bottles

- *DIY storage container for small items*

In this chapter, we will explore the potential of upcycling plastic lotion bottles to create DIY storage containers for small items. Plastic lotion bottles are a common household item that often gets discarded after use. However, with a little creativity and DIY skills, we can repurpose these bottles into practical and stylish storage solutions.

To begin, gather some empty plastic lotion bottles that are clean and dry. It's important to ensure that the bottles have been thoroughly washed and dried to remove any residue or odors. You can also remove any labels or sticker residues using soap and water or rubbing alcohol.

Next, decide on the design and purpose of your storage containers. Plastic lotion bottles come in various sizes and shapes, so consider how you plan to use them and what items you intend to store. For example, if you need a container for storing small craft supplies like beads or buttons, a smaller bottle with a narrow opening would be ideal.

Once you have determined the purpose and size of your storage container, it's time to get creative with the aesthetics. Consider painting the bottle using acrylic or spray paint to add a pop of color or to match your home decor. You can use stencils or masking tape to create patterns and designs. If you prefer a more natural look, consider using decoupage techniques to cover the bottle with fabric, paper, or even pressed flowers.

Now that your bottle is painted and decorated to your liking, it's time to think about the functionality. Depending on the size and shape of the bottle, you may need to make some modifications to transform it into a storage container. For instance, you can cut off the top of the bottle, leaving a rim to prevent items from falling out. If your bottle has a flip-top cap, you can remove it completely and attach a cork or a lid from another container to create a secure closure.

To enhance the functionality of your storage container, consider adding dividers or compartments inside the bottle. You can use cardboard or foam board to create partitions, allowing you to separate different types of small items. Alternatively, you can repurpose small plastic food containers or pill organizers and attach them inside the bottle to provide additional compartments.

Another idea is to attach hooks or clips to the outside of the bottle to hang it on a wall or a pegboard. This can be useful for storing nail polish or small tools. You can also attach magnets to the back of the bottle and use it on a magnetic surface, such as a refrigerator, to store lightweight metal items like paper clips or bobby pins.

By repurposing these bottles, not only are we reducing waste, but we are also adding a personal touch to our storage solutions. So go ahead and give it a try – unleash your DIY skills and transform those everyday plastic lotion bottles into functional and stylish storage containers!.

- Creating a soap dispenser

In the previous chapters of our book, we have explored the art of upcycling and repurposing various everyday items into functional and stylish creations. Now, in Chapter 5, we will delve into the realm of plastic lotion bottles and discover how to create a unique soap dispenser from this humble object.

Upcycling plastic lotion bottles into soap dispensers is a wonderful way to reduce waste and increase the functionality of these discarded containers. By following this step-by-step guide, you will be able to transform your lotion bottles into practical and aesthetically pleasing soap dispensers that will enhance your bathroom decor.

To begin this upcycling project, gather the following materials:

- Plastic lotion bottles (empty and clean).

- Soap pump mechanism (reusable or repurposed from old soap dispensers).

- Craft knife or scissors.

- Sandpaper or a nail file.

- Decorative elements (optional).

- Epoxy adhesive or a hot glue gun.

First, remove any remaining lotion from the bottle and rinse it thoroughly with warm water. Ensure that all residue is removed to prevent any unwanted scents or contamination in your soap dispenser.

Next, detach the pump mechanism from its current container, either by unscrewing it or by carefully removing it with a craft knife or scissors. Be cautious when using sharp tools and always prioritize safety.

Once you have the pump mechanism, measure the circumference of the lotion bottle's opening.

Use a craft knife or scissors to carefully cut a hole in the lid of the lotion bottle, ensuring that it is slightly smaller than the circumference of the pump mechanism. This will create a snug fit for the pump.

After cutting the hole, use sandpaper or a nail file to smooth any rough edges and create a clean opening. This step is vital to prevent any injuries when using the soap dispenser.

Now, it's time to attach the pump mechanism to the lotion bottle. Apply epoxy adhesive or use a hot glue gun to secure the pump in place. Ensure that it is centered and level to avoid any leaks or uneven dispensing of soap.

Once the adhesive has dried and the pump is firmly attached, test the dispenser by filling the bottle with your preferred liquid soap. Press the pump mechanism to check if the soap is being dispensed effectively. Make any necessary adjustments or repositioning of the pump if needed.

To add a personal and decorative touch to your soap dispenser, consider embellishing the lotion bottle. You can paint it with acrylic or spray paint, wrap it with decorative tape or fabric, or even glue on beads or buttons. Allow your creativity to shine and make this soap dispenser uniquely yours.

Finally, display your upcycled soap dispenser in your bathroom or kitchen, and enjoy the satisfaction of creating a functional and stylish piece from a plastic lotion bottle that would have otherwise been discarded.

By following the steps outlined in this guide, you can create a one-of-a-kind piece that not only reduces waste but also adds a touch of style to your living space. ".

- Lotion bottle herb garden

In this chapter, we will explore the possibilities of upcycling plastic lotion bottles and transforming them into a functional and stylish herb garden. By repurposing these everyday items, you can not only reduce waste but also create a beautiful display in your home that will provide fresh herbs for cooking and visual delight.

To begin, gather your materials. You will need plastic lotion bottles, scissors or a craft knife, potting soil, herb seeds or small herb plants, a drill or hot nail, and decorative materials such as twine or paint (optional).

Start by thoroughly cleaning the lotion bottles. Remove any labels or residue from the surface and rinse them with warm, soapy water. Ensure they are completely dry before proceeding.

Next, carefully cut off the top portion of the lotion bottle using scissors or a craft knife. This will serve as the main container for your herb garden. Consider adjusting the height of the container to your desired size, ensuring it is deep enough to hold the plants and soil.

Once the top portion is removed, create drainage holes at the bottom of the container. This is essential for preventing waterlogging and ensuring the herbs grow healthy. Use a drill or hot nail to make small holes in the bottom of the lotion bottle.

Now it's time to prepare the soil. Fill the container with potting soil, leaving enough space for the herb plants or seeds. Make sure the soil is well-drained and nutrient-rich to provide a suitable environment for your herbs to thrive.

If using seeds, follow the instructions on the seed packet for proper planting depth and spacing. Gently press the seeds into the soil and cover them lightly with more soil. If you prefer using small herb plants, carefully transplant them into the lotion bottle, ensuring the root system is covered with soil.

After planting, water the herb garden gently, making sure not to oversaturate the soil. Most herbs require around 6 hours of direct sunlight per day.

Alternatively, you can use paint to add vibrant colors or patterns to the container. Personalize it to suit your style and add visual interest to your space.

Remember to regularly water and tend to your herb garden. Keep an eye on the moisture levels and adjust accordingly, as different herbs have varying water requirements. Prune your herbs as needed to promote healthy growth and prevent overcrowding.

By following the steps outlined in this chapter, you can transform these everyday items into functional containers for growing herbs. Enjoy the process and the delights of having fresh herbs at your fingertips!.

Chapter 6: Repurposing Paper Towel Rolls

- Creating cord organizers

In this chapter, we will explore the exciting world of repurposing paper towel rolls to create innovative and functional cord organizers. These simple yet effective organizers provide a convenient and clutter-free solution to manage and store your cords. Let's dive into the step-by-step process of transforming paper towel rolls into unique cord organizers.

Step 1: Gather Materials.

To get started, you will need the following materials:

- Paper towel rolls: Collect a few empty paper towel rolls, making sure they are clean and dry before use.

- Scissors: A pair of sharp scissors will be handy for cutting the rolls.

- Decorative materials (optional): Explore your creativity by gathering decorative materials such as craft paper, washi tape, fabric, or stickers to add a personal touch to your cord organizers. This step is purely subjective and can be skipped if you prefer a minimalist look.

Step 2: Measure and Cut.

Begin by measuring the length of your cords. This will help determine the appropriate length for your cord organizers. Mark this length on the paper towel roll using a pen or a pencil. Once marked, use the scissors to carefully cut the roll along the marked line. Ensure that the cut is straight and clean for a professional finish.

Step 3: Organize and Tidy.

With the paper towel roll cut to the desired length, gather your cords and neatly wrap them around the roll. The hollow center of the roll provides an excellent storage space and keeps the cords tangle-free. For added convenience, you can label each cord organizer using stickers or small pieces of washi tape, indicating the type of cord contained within.

Step 4: Optional Decoration.

If you wish to add a decorative touch to your cord organizers, this is the perfect step to unleash your creativity. Using craft paper, washi tape, or fabric, wrap the paper towel roll in your chosen material. Secure the ends with glue or double-sided adhesive tape. Experiment with different patterns, colors, and textures to create a unique look for each cord organizer.

Step 5: Organize and Enjoy!.

Congratulations! You have successfully repurposed paper towel rolls into practical and visually appealing cord organizers. Arrange them in a drawer, on your desk, or anywhere you need to keep your cords organized and easily accessible. Not only will these organizers declutter your space, but they will also prevent cords from becoming tangled or lost.

By following the simple steps outlined above, you can transform everyday items into stylish and practical solutions for cord management. Start repurposing today and enjoy a clutter-free and organized living or workspace. Happy crafting!.

- Making seedling pots

This creative project allows you to give a second life to these otherwise disposable cardboard tubes, while also helping you save money on store-bought seedling containers.

To begin, gather your materials. You will need paper towel rolls, scissors, a ruler or measuring tape, a pencil or pen, potting soil, and your choice of seeds or seedlings.

First, measure and mark the desired length for each seedling pot on the paper towel rolls. A typical seedling pot size is around 2-3 inches in height, so mark the rolls accordingly.

Next, use your scissors to carefully cut along the marked lines. Take caution when cutting, as the cardboard can be a bit sturdy. Ensure that the cuts are clean and straight, as this will affect the stability of your seedling pots.

Once the rolls are cut, flatten each cardboard tube by gently pressing on it with your hands. This will make it easier to create the base of the seedling pots.

Now, fold one end of each flattened cardboard tube inward to create a bottom for the seedling pot. Press firmly to secure the fold in place. Make sure the bottom is flat and stable; otherwise, your seedlings may not grow properly.

With the base of the seedling pot created, it's time to fill it with potting soil. Carefully add enough soil so that it can accommodate the roots of your seedlings. Pat down lightly to ensure proper leveling.

Before planting the seeds or seedlings, moisten the soil slightly. This will provide the necessary moisture for the germination or growth of your plants.

Once the soil is moist, make small holes in the soil using your finger or a small dowel. Place the seeds or seedlings into the holes and cover them lightly with soil.

Water the newly planted seedlings gently and place them in a warm, well-lit area. Be sure to provide adequate daily care, such as regular watering and monitoring for any signs of pests or diseases.

As your seedlings grow and develop, the paper towel rolls will gradually decompose in the soil, allowing the roots to penetrate and establish themselves in the surrounding garden or larger pots. This natural decomposition is advantageous as it eliminates the need to remove the seedlings from their pots when it's time for transplantation.

Repurposing paper towel rolls into seedling pots is not only an eco-friendly option, but it also adds a charming touch to your gardening endeavors. With a little creativity and resourcefulness, you can transform these humble cardboard tubes into functional and stylish containers for your seedlings.

Remember to experiment with different sizes or decorations to personalize your seedling pots further. This simple DIY project is not only rewarding, but it also showcases the value of repurposing everyday items for a more sustainable lifestyle. Enjoy the process and happy gardening!.

- Paper towel roll wall art

As a skilled artisan in DIY productions, I am excited to share with you a detailed guide on creating an interesting and stylish piece of wall art using paper towel rolls. This upcycling project not only allows you to repurpose everyday items, but also adds a touch of creativity to your living space. So, let's dive right in!.

To start off, gather the following materials for this project:

- Paper towel rolls (collected from your household).

- Scissors.

- Ruler.

- Pencil.

- Craft glue or hot glue gun.

- Paint (acrylic or spray paint).

- Paintbrush (optional).

- Decorative embellishments (such as beads, buttons, or ribbon).

Step 1: Flatten and cut the rolls.

Take the paper towel rolls and flatten them by pressing them with your hands. This will make it easier to work with. Once flat, use a pair of scissors to cut the rolls into smaller sections. The size of these sections will depend on your desired design and the dimensions of the wall space where you plan to hang the art.

Step 2: Plan your design.

Using a ruler and a pencil, mark the desired length of each section on the cut paper towel rolls. Take into consideration the overall shape and pattern you want to create. This step will help ensure that all the sections are uniform in size and shape.

Step 3: Shape the sections.

Now, it's time to get creative! Use your scissors to cut different shapes out of each marked section. You can experiment with various designs like flowers, leaves, or abstract shapes. Don't be afraid to let your imagination run wild!.

Step 4: Paint.

Once you have shaped all the sections according to your desired design, it's time to add some color. Use acrylic paint or spray paint to paint the sections in your chosen colors. This step is optional, but it can add an extra pop to your wall art. Feel free to use a paintbrush or simply dip each section in a bowl of paint for a more rustic look.

Step 5: Arrange and glue.

After the paint has dried, it's time to arrange the sections in your desired composition. Play around with different layouts until you find the perfect arrangement. Once satisfied, use craft glue or a hot glue gun to securely attach the sections to each other. .

Step 6: Add embellishments (optional).

To add a personal touch and some extra flair to your wall art, consider adding decorative embellishments like beads, buttons, or ribbon. This step is entirely optional, but it can bring a unique and eye-catching element to your creation.

Step 7: Hang your masterpiece.

Choose a suitable spot on your wall, use nails or adhesive hooks to hang it up, and step back to admire your beautiful creation!.

By following these steps and letting your imagination soar, you can transform simple everyday items into functional and stylish creations. Remember, the possibilities are endless when it comes to DIY projects like this one. Enjoy the process and embrace the satisfaction of creating something beautiful from items that might have otherwise ended up in the trash. Happy crafting!.

Chapter 7: Upcycling Toilet Paper Rolls

- DIY drawer organizers

These simple yet effective organizing solutions will not only help you declutter your drawers, but also add a touch of eco-friendliness to your home. So, let's dive into the world of upcycling and repurposing!.

Toilet paper rolls are one of the most versatile and readily available materials for upcycling. With a little creativity and some basic tools, you can turn these humble containers into beautiful organizers for your drawers. Here's how:

1. Preparing the toilet paper rolls: Start by gathering a collection of toilet paper rolls. Make sure

to remove any lingering tissues and flatten the rolls for easier handling. It's also a good idea to trim the rolls to your desired length, depending on the dimensions of your drawer.

2. Decorating the rolls: Now comes the fun part - decorating the rolls! You can get as creative as you like with this step. Consider using paint, decorative papers, fabric, or even washi tape to add a splash of color and style to your organizers. Let your imagination run wild and experiment with different patterns and designs.

3. Securing the rolls: Once your rolls are beautifully decorated, it's time to secure them together. Place the rolls in the desired configuration and use adhesive materials such as glue or double-sided tape to hold them together. This will create a sturdy structure that can easily be placed inside your drawer.

4. Customizing the compartments: To make the organizers even more functional, consider customizing the compartments based on your

specific needs. You can achieve this by cutting or folding the roll in various ways. For example, if you need larger sections for storing bulkier items, you can cut the roll lengthwise and create wider compartments. Similarly, folding the roll in half can create smaller sections for storing tiny items like jewelry or small stationery supplies.

5. You can use them for a wide range of items, such as office supplies, kitchen utensils, makeup, or even jewelry. The possibilities are endless!.

Give these ideas a try and let your creativity shine as you transform everyday items into functional and sustainable creations.

Remember, upcycling and repurposing is all about finding new ways to breathe life into old objects. So, instead of throwing them away, consider how you can give them a new purpose. In the following chapters, we will explore numerous other materials that can be upcycled and repurposed into useful creations. Stay tuned for more inspiration and practical ideas!.

It does not explain any other topics or repeat question information.

- Crafting mini gift boxes

One creative and eco-friendly way to repurpose everyday items is by upcycling toilet paper rolls into charming mini gift boxes. These mini gift boxes are not only practical, but they also add a personal touch to any gift or occasion. In this chapter, we will explore the step-by-step process of transforming toilet paper rolls into beautiful mini gift boxes.

To begin, gather all the necessary materials. Apart from toilet paper rolls, you will need scissors, craft paper or wrapping paper, a ruler, a pencil, a glue stick or adhesive, and decorative embellishments such as ribbons, stickers, or bows. These materials can easily be sourced from your DIY crafting supplies or repurposed from items you may already have at home.

Start by flattening the toilet paper roll and marking the desired height for your mini gift box using a ruler and pencil. Once you have marked the height, cut the toilet paper roll to create a cylinder. Remember to handle scissors with care and keep them away from children.

Next, cover the outside of the toilet paper roll cylinder with craft paper or wrapping paper of your choice. Measure and cut the paper to fit the circumference of the cylinder, leaving some excess on both ends. Apply glue or adhesive to the inside of the paper, and carefully wrap it around the toilet paper roll, pressing firmly to ensure it sticks.

Once the paper is securely attached, fold and tuck the excess paper at both ends of the cylinder into the open ends. This creates the closed bottom and top of the gift box. Use glue or adhesive to secure these folds in place.

Now that the basic structure of the mini gift box is complete, it's time to add the finishing touches. Get creative with embellishments such as ribbons, stickers, bows, or any other decorative items you have on hand. You can also personalize the gift box by adding the recipient's name or a custom message using markers or calligraphy pens.

These mini gift boxes made from upcycled toilet paper rolls are not only suitable for small items like jewelry or chocolates, but they can also be customized to accommodate a variety of gift sizes. By varying the height and width of the paper roll cylinders, you can create mini gift boxes for anything from delicate trinkets to small gadgets.

Remember, upcycling and repurposing everyday items is not only a fun and creative activity but also plays a significant role in reducing waste and promoting sustainability. By adopting a DIY approach to crafting, you are contributing towards a greener and more eco-conscious lifestyle.

In summary, transforming toilet paper rolls into mini gift boxes is a simple yet delightful DIY project. By repurposing these everyday items, you can create unique and stylish packaging for your gifts while reducing waste. So, gather your materials, follow the steps outlined in this chapter, and let your creativity shine as you craft these charming mini gift boxes from upcycled toilet paper rolls. Happy crafting!.

- Toilet paper roll bird feeder

In this chapter, we will be exploring various ways to upcycle and repurpose toilet paper rolls. This project allows you to transform a simple household item into a functional and stylish addition to your outdoor space. Let's dive straight into the instructions!.

To begin, gather all the necessary materials for your bird feeder project. These include toilet paper rolls, peanut butter (or any sticky substance like honey or almond butter), birdseed, a string or twine, and a pair of scissors.

1. Start by cutting a long piece of string or twine, around 12 inches in length. This will be used to hang the bird feeder.

2. Next, take one toilet paper roll and measure approximately 2 inches from the top. Using the pair of scissors, carefully make two small holes on opposite sides of the roll at this marked point. These holes will serve as the entry points for the string or twine, allowing you to hang the feeder.

3. After making the holes, thread the string or twine through them, making sure both ends of the string come out of the top of the roll. Tie a secure knot at the ends to create a loop, forming the hanger for your bird feeder.

4. Once the hanger is in place, smear generous amounts of peanut butter (or your chosen sticky substance) around the entire outside surface of the toilet paper roll. This will act as a glue to hold the birdseed onto the feeder. If you're using multiple rolls, repeat this step for each.

5. Pour birdseed onto a flat surface or plate. Roll each peanut butter-coated toilet paper roll carefully in the birdseed, ensuring all sides are covered. Gently press the birdseed onto the surface of the roll to make sure it adheres well. Repeat this process for each roll.

6. Once the rolls are completely coated with birdseed, find a suitable location to hang your bird feeder. It could be a tree branch, a hook on a fence, or any other place visible to birds.

7. Carefully hang your bird feeder using the loop you created earlier. Make sure it is securely fastened and at a height that is easily accessible for the birds.

Now, sit back and enjoy the sight of birds flocking to your DIY creation! Remember to periodically check and refill the birdseed to keep the feathered visitors happy and well-fed.

By upcycling toilet paper rolls into a bird feeder, you have not only reduced waste but also provided a practical and decorative addition to your outdoor space. This project showcases the endless possibilities of upcycling and repurposing everyday items. Get creative, experiment with different materials, and enjoy the satisfaction of transforming something ordinary into something extraordinary.

Additionally, be cautious of the location you choose to hang your bird feeder, considering any potential hazards that may endanger the birds or disrupt their feeding process.

Chapter 8: Repurposing Plastic Grocery Bags

- Creating woven mats or rugs

This DIY project not only allows you to engage in a creative endeavor but also helps in reducing plastic waste.

To begin, gather all the plastic grocery bags you have accumulated. Make sure they are clean and free from any food residue or stains. It's important to reuse materials responsibly and to prepare them adequately for repurposing.

The first step in creating your woven mat or rug is to prepare the plastic grocery bags by flattening and folding them into strips. Start by cutting off the handles and bottom portion of the bag, so you're left with a rectangular piece. Fold the rectangular piece lengthwise and continue folding until you achieve a strip of the desired width. Repeat this process with several bags until you have enough strips to create your mat.

Next, it's time to start weaving. Choose a flat surface, such as a table or a large tray, to serve as your weaving platform. If necessary, cover the surface with a protective layer, such as a plastic sheet or an old tablecloth, to avoid any potential damage.

To initiate the weaving process, take two of your prepared plastic strips and place them perpendicular to each other on the weaving platform, creating a cross shape. Use tape or small weights to secure them in place temporarily.

Now, take another plastic strip and weave it under the horizontal strip and over the vertical strip. Repeat this process, alternating between over and under, until the strip reaches the end. Secure the strip by either tying a knot at the end or using a small piece of tape. Repeat this step with additional strips until you have created several rows.

To add more color and texture to your woven mat or rug, consider incorporating different colored plastic strips or even creating patterns by strategically placing contrasting strips. Get creative and let your imagination run wild.

Continue weaving and adding strips until your mat or rug reaches the desired size. It's important to maintain a consistent tension and tightness throughout the weaving process to ensure a sturdy and durable final product.

Once you've finished weaving, secure the edges of your mat or rug to prevent it from unraveling. You can use a needle and thread to sew along the edges or even glue them for added reinforcement.

Lastly, give your woven mat or rug a thorough clean. As plastic can attract dust and dirt, it's essential to keep your creation looking fresh and vibrant. Use a damp cloth or sponge to wipe down the surface, and for tougher stains, a gentle soap solution should do the trick.

Now you have a beautiful and functional woven mat or rug created entirely from repurposed plastic grocery bags. Not only did you divert waste from the landfill, but you also transformed everyday items into a stylish and unique home decor piece.

- *Plastic bag organizers*

Plastic grocery bags are one of the most commonly accumulated items in households, and it's important to find creative ways to reuse them and reduce waste.

To create a plastic bag organizer, you will need the following supplies: plastic grocery bags, a pair of scissors, a ruler, a sewing needle, and thread. The ultimate goal is to create a handy storage solution that allows you to neatly store and access your plastic bags.

To begin, flatten out a plastic grocery bag and smooth out any wrinkles. Lay it on a flat surface and cut off the bottom of the bag. Then, fold the bottom of the bag up to meet the top, creating a rectangular shape.

Next, using a ruler, measure and mark 1-inch intervals along the folded side of the bag. This will serve as a guide for where to make your cuts to create strips. Once marked, carefully cut along the marked lines, creating a series of long strips.

Now, unfold the bag and you will notice that it is divided into long, connected loops. Take one of the loops and stretch it gently; this will create a longer strip. Repeat this step with all the loops, stretching them one by one.

Take one of the strips and tie a knot at one end. This will act as a stopper to prevent the plastic bags from sliding off. Then, take another strip and weave it through the first strip, going over and under, creating a simple weaving pattern. Continue weaving until you reach the end of the first strip.

Repeat the weaving process, adding more strips as needed, until you reach your desired length. This will create a net-like structure that allows you to easily insert and remove plastic bags.

Once you have completed the weaving, secure the loose ends of the strips by tying them in a knot. Trim any excess length if desired. Your plastic bag organizer is now ready to use!.

Hang the organizer in a convenient location, such as a closet or pantry door, using a hook or adhesive. This will keep your plastic bags organized and easily accessible whenever you need them.

By repurposing plastic grocery bags into a functional plastic bag organizer, you are not only reducing waste but also creating a practical solution for organizing your home. Get creative and experiment with different colors and patterns of plastic bags to add a unique touch to your organizer.

Remember, upcycling and repurposing everyday items is a great way to save money, reduce waste, and unleash your creativity. So go ahead, gather your supplies, and enjoy the satisfaction of turning a simple plastic grocery bag into a stylish and practical storage solution.

- DIY raincoat or poncho

Using your creativity and a few simple steps, you'll be able to transform these plastic bags into a practical and stylish outerwear option.

To begin the process, gather a sufficient number of plastic grocery bags. The exact number will depend on the size of your raincoat or poncho and the thickness of the bags. Make sure the bags are clean and free from any stains or food residue, as this will directly affect the final appearance of your creation.

Next, prepare your work surface by laying down a protective covering or old cloth to prevent any damage or mess. It's always a good idea to work in a well-ventilated area to minimize contact with any dust or fumes.

Now, carefully cut off the handles and bottom seams of the plastic bags. This will create separate rectangular pieces of plastic that can be used to construct your raincoat or poncho. It's important to note that the size of each piece will determine the overall size of your raincoat or poncho, so adjust accordingly.

Once you have enough plastic pieces, it's time to assemble them. Lay them out flat in a pattern that you find appealing. You can be as creative as you like, arranging the pieces in different colors or even adding in other repurposed materials such as glass bottles, aluminum cans, or wine corks for added style and interest. Secure the pieces together using strong adhesive tape or by heat sealing the edges with an iron set on low heat.

As you assemble the plastic pieces, consider adding additional features to your raincoat or poncho. For example, you can create a hood by cutting a separate piece of plastic in a shape that fits comfortably over your head. This will provide protection from the rain, keeping you dry and stylish at the same time.

Make any necessary adjustments by trimming excess material or adding more plastic pieces until you achieve the desired size and shape.

Finally, take your completed raincoat or poncho outside and put it to the test. Brave the rain, knowing that you not only created a functional protective garment but also repurposed materials that may have otherwise ended up in the landfill. Feel proud of your contribution to sustainability and fashion!.

Remember, the possibilities for repurposing plastic grocery bags are endless. This guide serves as a starting point for your creative endeavors, but don't be afraid to experiment and add your own unique touch. Upcycling and repurposing not only helps reduce waste but also allows you to express your personal style and creativity in a sustainable way.

Chapter 9: Repurposing Plastic Food Packaging

- *Creating mini storage containers*

Repurposing plastic food packaging is a great way to reduce waste and create practical storage solutions for your home. In this chapter, we will focus specifically on repurposing plastic shower curtains, plastic laundry detergent bottles, plastic shampoo bottles, plastic lotion bottles, paper towel rolls, toilet paper rolls, plastic grocery bags, plastic food packaging, plastic clamshell containers, plastic takeout containers, plastic egg cartons, plastic milk jugs, plastic soda bottles, wine corks, wine bottles, glass jars, glass bottles, tin cans, aluminum cans, and paper bags.

To create mini storage containers out of plastic food packaging, you will need the following materials:

1. Plastic shower curtains: To repurpose a plastic shower curtain into a mini storage container, start by cutting it into smaller, manageable pieces. Then fold and stitch the edges to create a simple pouch-like container. You can customize the size and shape of your containers depending on your storage needs.

2. Plastic laundry detergent bottles, plastic shampoo bottles, and plastic lotion bottles: These plastic bottles can be transformed into mini storage containers by cutting off the top portion and cleaning the inside thoroughly. You can then use them to store small items such as jewelry or office supplies. To enhance the aesthetics, you can paint or decorate the bottles according to your preference.

3. Paper towel rolls and toilet paper rolls: Paper towel and toilet paper rolls can be upcycled into mini storage containers by cutting them into shorter segments. Seal one end of each segment by folding and taping it. You can use these containers to store small accessories like hair ties, buttons, or paper clips.

4. Plastic grocery bags: To repurpose plastic grocery bags into mini storage containers, start by flattening the bag and folding it into a square or rectangular shape. Fold the sides inward and create creases. Then fold the bottom and top parts inward to form a pouch-like container. Secure the sides with tape or glue, and your mini storage container is ready to use.

5. Plastic clamshell containers and plastic takeout containers: These containers can be repurposed as mini storage compartments by cleaning them thoroughly and removing any stickers or labels. You can utilize them to store small craft items, buttons, or even office supplies. If desired, you can also paint or decorate the containers to match your décor.

6. Plastic egg cartons: Plastic egg cartons can serve as excellent mini storage containers for small items. Clean the egg carton thoroughly, making sure to remove any remaining eggshell or residue. Each compartment in the egg carton can provide separate

storage space for earrings, rings, or other small accessories.

7. Plastic milk jugs and plastic soda bottles: Repurpose these plastic containers into mini storage solutions by cutting off the top section and cleaning them thoroughly. You can divide the containers into smaller sections by cutting them lengthwise or crosswise and create individual storage compartments. They can be used to store small items like screws, nails, or beads.

8. Wine corks: Wine corks can be transformed into mini storage containers by cutting them in half or drilling a hole through the center. You can use them to store small items like sewing needles, pins, or even small pieces of jewelry. Arrange the corks in a box or container to keep them organized.

9. Wine bottles, glass jars, tin cans, aluminum cans, and paper bags: These items can be repurposed into mini storage containers by cleaning them thoroughly and removing any labels or stickers. Wine bottles and glass jars can be used to hold small-sized

items like cotton balls or Q-tips in the bathroom or as organizers on shelves. Tin cans and aluminum cans can be decorated and utilized as pen holders or for storing small tools. Paper bags can be folded and stapled to create pouch-like storage containers for various purposes.

By using everyday items like plastic shower curtains, plastic bottles, paper towel and toilet paper rolls, plastic grocery bags, plastic food packaging, plastic clamshell containers, plastic takeout containers, plastic egg cartons, plastic milk jugs, plastic soda bottles, wine corks, wine bottles, glass jars, glass bottles, tin cans, aluminum cans, and paper bags, you can create customized storage solutions that are both functional and stylish. Remember to clean and prepare the materials properly before repurposing them, and feel free to add your own creative touches through painting or decorating. Happy upcycling!.

- Making a DIY wallet

In this chapter, we will explore the creative and practical possibilities of repurposing plastic food packaging to make a DIY wallet. Plastic food packaging is something we encounter on a daily basis, and often discard without realizing its potential for repurposing. By upcycling these items, we can reduce waste and create functional and stylish creations.

Let's begin with plastic shower curtains. These can be transformed into durable and waterproof wallets. Cut the shower curtain into the desired size and shape for your wallet. Fold it in half, ensuring that the design side is facing inward. Sew the sides together using a strong thread or a sewing machine. Leave the top open to create a pocket for your belongings. You can add a button or a Velcro closure to secure the wallet. By repurposing a plastic shower curtain, you not only create a unique wallet but also give it a water-resistant advantage.

Next, we have plastic laundry detergent, shampoo, and lotion bottles. These bottles are often made of sturdy plastic and can be upcycled into practical and durable wallets. Start by cleaning and drying the bottles thoroughly. Cut off the top and bottom sections, leaving a rectangular piece of plastic. Flatten the plastic and fold it in half. Apply heat using an iron or a heat gun to seal the edges, creating a pocket for your wallet. You can get creative by adding additional pockets or compartments using smaller pieces of plastic. Attach a closure of your choice, such as Velcro or a snap button, to keep your belongings secure.

Moving on, let's explore the possibilities of paper towel and toilet paper rolls. These cylindrical cardboard tubes can be transformed into unique and eco-friendly wallets. Start by flattening the rolls and cutting them into smaller sections. Arrange the sections in a pattern of your choice to create the desired shape and size for your wallet. Use glue or tape to secure the sections together, ensuring that the edges align. You can further embellish the wallet by covering it with fabric or decorative paper. Add a closure, such as a ribbon or a clip, to keep your belongings safe.

Plastic grocery bags are another material that can be repurposed into a DIY wallet. Begin by flattening the bag and cutting off the handles and the bottom. Cut open one side of the bag to create a rectangular sheet of plastic. Fold the plastic in half and sew the sides together, leaving the top open. You can reinforce the wallet by sewing along the edges several times. Attach a closure, such as a zipper or a button, to complete your recycled plastic grocery bag wallet.

Plastic food packaging such as plastic clamshell containers and takeout containers can also be repurposed into stylish wallets. Start by cleaning and drying the containers thoroughly. Cut off the desired section of plastic and trim it to the desired shape for your wallet. Fold the plastic in half and sew the sides together. Leave the top open to create a pocket for your belongings. Enhance the look of your wallet by adding embellishments such as buttons or beads. Plastic egg cartons and plastic milk jugs can also be utilized in a similar manner to create unique and eco-friendly wallets.

By upcycling materials that would have otherwise been thrown away, we can reduce waste and contribute to a more sustainable lifestyle. Whether it's transforming plastic shower curtains, laundry detergent bottles, or even paper towel rolls, the possibilities for creating stylish wallets are only limited by your imagination. So go ahead and unleash your creativity, and enjoy the process of transforming everyday items into functional and fashionable creations. Happy wallet-making!.

- Plastic packaging planters

In this chapter, we will explore the creative process of repurposing plastic food packaging into unique and functional planters. Plastic packaging is a common material that often goes to waste after its initial use. However, with a little imagination and some simple DIY techniques, we can transform these materials into beautiful and eco-friendly planters that will not only enhance the aesthetic appeal of your space but also contribute to a more sustainable lifestyle.

Plastic food packaging comes in various shapes and sizes, such as clamshell containers, takeout containers, egg cartons, and milk jugs. Each of these containers has unique characteristics that can be harnessed when repurposed into planters.

To begin, collect an assortment of plastic food packaging that you have accumulated over time. Thoroughly clean and dry each container before proceeding. Cleaning the containers ensures that any food residue is removed, reducing the chances of attracting pests or contaminating your plants.

Once the containers are clean and dry, it's time to unleash your creativity. Depending on the shape and size of the container, you can either use it as it is or choose to modify it to suit your desired planter design.

For containers such as clamshell containers, takeout containers, and egg cartons, you may need to drill or cut drainage holes at the bottom. Proper drainage is essential for any planter to prevent waterlogging, which can lead to root rot. Use a drill or a sharp utility knife to create a few small holes evenly spaced across the bottom of the container.

Plastic milk jugs and soda bottles can be repurposed into hanging planters. Use a pair of sharp scissors or a craft knife to carefully cut out a section from the side of the container, leaving a wide opening. You can then attach ropes or chains to create your hanging planter.

For plastic grocery bags and food packaging, you can repurpose them into self-watering planters. Cut off the bottom of the bag or packaging and fill it with a layer of small stones or pebbles. This will act as a reservoir for water. Place a piece of fabric or a wick, such as a cotton string or a shoelace, into the water reservoir and let it rest on the pebbles. Fill the rest of the container with potting soil and plant your chosen greenery. Water can be added to the reservoir, and the plant will draw water as needed through the wick, ensuring proper hydration and reducing the frequency of watering.

Once your plastic food packaging has been repurposed into planters, it's time to unleash your creativity by decorating them. You can paint the planters with acrylic paint, use decoupage techniques with fabric or paper, or even experiment with different textures and materials such as stones or seashells. The possibilities are endless, and the results can be truly spectacular.

Remember, the key to successful upcycling and repurposing is to let your imagination soar and see the hidden potential in everyday items. By repurposing plastic food packaging into planters, you not only reduce waste but also give these materials a new lease on life. The end result will not only be aesthetically pleasing but will also serve as a reminder of the value of sustainable living.

In the next chapter, we will explore another exciting repurposing project using shower curtains. Stay tuned!.

Chapter 10: Upcycling Plastic Clamshell Containers

- *Creating a travel jewelry case*

This DIY project allows you to repurpose an item that would otherwise be discarded, giving it a new life and purpose.

To begin, gather all the materials you will need for this project. Besides the plastic clamshell containers, gather a pair of scissors or a utility knife, strong glue or adhesive, colorful patterned fabric or adhesive paper, decorative elements such as ribbons or buttons, a marker or pen, and a ruler or measuring tape.

The first step in reusing a plastic clamshell container as a jewelry case is to clean and remove any labels or stickers from the surface. Wash the container with warm soapy water, ensuring it is free of any residue or dirt. Let it dry completely before proceeding to the next step.

Once the container is clean and dry, you can start the transformation process. Take your scissors or utility knife and carefully cut the top lid of the clamshell container, separating it from the base. Make sure to cut along the existing hinge line to create a clean and neat separation.

Next, take the bottom half of the clamshell container and measure the interior dimensions. Use a ruler or measuring tape to measure the length, width, and depth. This will help you determine the size of the fabric or adhesive paper you will need to cover the inside of the container.

Once you have the measurements, mark them on the fabric or adhesive paper using a pen or marker. Cut the fabric or paper with scissors, ensuring it is slightly larger than the measured dimensions to allow for a snug fit inside the container.

Apply a layer of strong glue or adhesive to the bottom interior of the container. Carefully place the fabric or adhesive paper on top of the glue, pressing it down gently to secure it in place. Smooth out any wrinkles or air bubbles with your hand or a small roller.

For added durability and a polished look, you can also apply a layer of glue or adhesive on top of the fabric or paper once it is in place. This will help protect it from wear and tear over time.

Now that the interior of the jewelry case is complete, focus on the exterior to make it visually appealing. You can choose to decorate the outside of the container with colorful adhesive paper, fabric, or by painting it with acrylic paints.

Furthermore, consider adding decorative elements such as ribbons, buttons, or beads to the edges or top of the clamshell container. These embellishments will enhance the overall aesthetic and give a personal touch to your travel jewelry case.

Once you are satisfied with the appearance of your jewelry case, let it dry completely before using it to store your jewelry items. It is now ready to accompany you on your future travels and keep your precious accessories organized and protected.

By following the steps outlined in this guide, you can transform a simple container into a functional and stylish storage solution for your jewelry. Don't forget to experiment with different materials and decorations to make it uniquely yours. Happy crafting!.

- DIY succulent planter

Upcycling is a wonderful way to breathe new life into ordinary items, ultimately reducing waste and creating unique and charming pieces for your home. In this chapter, we will provide a detailed guide and step-by-step instructions to help you on your creative journey.

Plastic clamshell containers, often used for packaging products such as fruits, vegetables, and small electronic items, can be easily repurposed as planters for succulents. Succulents are low-maintenance plants that require minimal watering, making them ideal for any DIY project. By upcycling these containers, you can create a beautiful and sustainable display for your succulents.

To begin this DIY project, you will need the following materials:

1. Plastic clamshell containers - Choose containers without any cracks or damage, ensuring that they are clean and free from any residue. It is advisable to select containers with clear lids for better visibility of the succulents.

2. Succulent plants - Select a variety of succulents with different colors, shapes, and sizes to create an eye-catching display. Visit your local plant nursery or garden center to choose the plants that best suit your design preferences.

3. Potting soil - Succulents thrive in well-draining soil, so opt for potting soil specifically formulated for cacti and succulents. You can find this type of soil at your nearest gardening store.

4. Pebbles or gravel - These will be used for drainage purposes. Choose small pebbles or gravel that will fit inside the clamshell containers.

5. Decorative elements (optional) - If you want to add a personal touch to your succulent planters, you can gather decorative elements such as small figurines, seashells, or colored stones.

1. Start by thoroughly cleaning the plastic clamshell containers. Remove any stickers, adhesive residue, or dirt to ensure a clean and attractive look.

2. Using a small drill or a pointed object like a pen or skewer, create drainage holes in the bottom of the containers. These holes will allow excess

water to escape, preventing root rot and maintaining the health of your succulents.

3. Place a layer of pebbles or gravel at the bottom of each container. This layer will prevent water from accumulating and creating a soggy environment for the succulents.

4. Fill the containers with the potting soil, leaving a small space at the top for the succulents to sit comfortably. Gently pat down the soil to ensure stability.

5. Carefully take out the succulents from their original pots, ensuring that their roots are intact. Place the succulents into the containers, arranging them in a visually pleasing manner. You can mix different varieties to create an interesting and vibrant display.

6. Once all the succulents are in place, add more potting soil around them, gently pressing it down with your fingers to secure the plants in position.

7. Water the succulents lightly, being careful not to overwater. Succulents thrive in dry conditions, so it is better to err on the side of caution when watering them.

8. If desired, add decorative elements to enhance the overall look of the succulent planters. Arrange figurines, seashells, or colored stones around the succulents to create a personalized touch.

9. Succulents thrive in areas with bright, indirect sunlight, so make sure to place them near a window or in a well-lit spot in your home. Also, keep in mind that succulents prefer warmer temperatures, so avoid exposing them to drafts or extreme cold.

10.

By following the step-by-step instructions provided in this chapter, you can transform these discarded containers into functional and stylish planters that showcase the beauty of succulent plants. So, gather your materials, let your creativity flow, and embark on this exciting upcycling adventure!.

- *Plastic clamshell organizer*

Plastic clamshell containers are commonly used for packaging various products, such as electronics, toys, and household items. Instead of throwing them away, we can transform these containers into a useful organizer that can help keep our belongings neat and organized.

To start, gather all the necessary materials and tools for this project. You will need plastic clamshell containers, a hot glue gun, scissors, decorative paper or fabric (optional), and any other embellishments you desire (such as ribbons, buttons, or stickers). .

First, thoroughly clean the plastic clamshell containers to remove any residue or stickers. You can use warm soapy water and a sponge for this step. Make sure to dry them completely before continuing.

Next, carefully cut the clamshell containers into desired sizes and shapes. Depending on the size of the containers, you may choose to cut them into smaller individual compartments or leave them as larger sections. This will depend on your specific organizational needs.

Once the containers are cut, you can choose to cover them with decorative paper or fabric to give them a more personalized and stylish look. Simply measure the dimensions of each section and cut the paper or fabric accordingly. Attach the covering using a hot glue gun, making sure it is secure and neat.

Now it's time to assemble the organizer. Arrange the covered plastic clamshell containers in a way that suits your storage needs. You can stack them vertically or horizontally, depending on the space you have available. Use the hot glue gun to secure them together, making sure they are sturdy and stable.

If desired, you can further enhance the organizer by adding additional embellishments. Attach ribbons, buttons, or stickers to the exterior of the containers to give them a unique and artistic touch.

Place it on a tabletop, desk, or inside a drawer to keep your small items like jewelry, office supplies, or craft materials neatly organized.

The great thing about this upcycling project is that you can easily customize it to meet your specific needs. You can create compartments of different sizes, add dividers, or even paint the containers in your favorite colors. Let your creativity flow and make it a reflection of your personal style.

By repurposing plastic clamshell containers into a functional organizer, you not only contribute to the reduction of waste but also create a unique and useful item for your home. With a little time and creativity, you can transform these everyday items into stylish and functional creations. Enjoy the satisfaction of repurposing materials and adding a touch of personalization to your living space.

Chapter 11: Repurposing Plastic Takeout Containers

- Lunchbox from takeout containers

Upcycling and repurposing everyday items is not only a great way to reduce waste and save money, but it also allows you to tap into your creative side and create functional and stylish pieces that can be used in your day-to-day life. In this chapter, we will focus on repurposing plastic takeout containers into a DIY lunchbox.

Plastic takeout containers are an excellent material for upcycling projects due to their durability and versatility. To create a lunchbox from these containers, you will need a few supplies and follow these simple steps.

1. Gather your materials: You will need a plastic takeout container, a ruler, a marker, a cutting tool (such as scissors or a utility knife), sandpaper, non-toxic paint, a paintbrush, and some adhesive Velcro straps.

2. Prepare your container: Start by removing any residual food or grease from the takeout container. Wash it thoroughly with warm water and gentle soap. Once it's dry, trim off any excess parts of the container that you don't need for your lunchbox, such as handles or unnecessary compartments.

3. Measure and mark the dimensions: Use a ruler and marker to measure and mark the dimensions you want for your lunchbox. Consider the size of your usual lunch items and make sure the container will accommodate them comfortably.

4. Cut the container: Carefully cut along the marked lines using your cutting tool. Take your time and ensure clean and straight edges. You can smooth

any rough edges using sandpaper, creating a polished finish.

5. Decorate your lunchbox: Now comes the fun part – decorating your lunchbox! Use non-toxic paint to give your lunchbox a personal touch. You can experiment with different colors, patterns, or even add some stickers or stencils to make it unique.

6. Add closures: To keep your lunch securely closed, attach adhesive Velcro straps to the edges of the container. This will provide a reliable closure while still allowing for easy access to your lunch.

Once your DIY lunchbox is complete, make sure to test it out before using it on a daily basis. Load it up with your favorite lunch items and ensure that it can hold everything securely without any spillage.

With just a few simple steps, some creativity, and the right supplies, you can create a practical and stylish lunchbox that you'll be proud to use every day. So, channel your inner artisan and start upcycling today!.

- DIY planters for herbs or flowers

With just a few simple steps, you can transform these otherwise disposable containers into beautiful and functional planters that will not only add a touch of nature to your space but also help reduce waste. Let's dive into the process!.

To begin, gather your materials. You will need a plastic takeout container, a utility knife, a marker or pen, potting soil, and your choice of herb or flower seeds or seedlings. It's important to note that plastic takeout containers come in various shapes and sizes, so choose one that is suitable for the kind of plant you wish to grow.

Once you have your materials ready, start by cleaning the takeout container thoroughly. Remove any leftover food or residue and wash it with warm soapy water. Make sure to rinse it thoroughly to get rid of any soap residue. .

Next, use a marker or pen to draw a line across the container, about 2 inches from the bottom. This will serve as a cutting guide. Using a utility knife, carefully cut along this line to separate the bottom part of the container from the top. Set the top part aside, as we will only be using the bottom portion for our planter.

Now that you have the bottom part of the takeout container, it's time to prepare it for planting. Using the utility knife, poke a few small drainage holes in the bottom. This will prevent water from pooling at the bottom and ensure proper drainage for your plants.

Fill the container with potting soil, leaving about an inch of space from the top. Gently pat down the soil to create a firm base for your plants. If you're using seeds, follow the packet instructions for planting depth and spacing. If you have seedlings, carefully transplant them into the container, making sure to gently loosen and tease their roots for better growth.

Once your plants are securely planted in the container, water them thoroughly. Make sure the soil is evenly moist but not waterlogged. Place the planter in a spot that receives adequate sunlight for the specific plant you're growing. Provide regular watering and appropriate care according to the plant's needs.

One of the advantages of repurposing plastic takeout containers as planters is their portability. You can easily move them around as needed or place them in different areas of your home, balcony, or garden. Additionally, the transparent nature of many takeout containers allows you to observe the growth of your plants and monitor their moisture levels.

It's a simple yet impactful way to incorporate greenery into your surroundings while adding a personal touch. Let your creativity shine as you experiment with different plants, container sizes, and arrangements to create a delightful and sustainable garden. Happy repurposing!.

- *Takeout container drawer dividers*

Using plastic takeout containers to organize your drawers not only helps you declutter your space but also gives these single-use items a new purpose in your home. With a few simple steps and some creativity, you can transform these containers into useful and stylish drawer dividers.

To start, gather your materials. You will need clean plastic takeout containers, a pair of scissors, a ruler or measuring tape, a marker or pen, and adhesive materials such as glue or double-sided tape. Choose containers with heights that match the depth of your drawer to ensure a snug fit.

First, measure the width and length of your drawer. Use these measurements to cut the plastic containers accordingly. Mark the outlines of the dividers on the containers, ensuring that there is ample space between each section to accommodate the items you'll be storing.

Next, use the scissors to carefully cut along the marked lines. Take your time and make precise cuts to ensure neat and even dividers. Smooth out any rough edges with sandpaper or a nail file if desired.

Now, it's time to assemble the dividers. Arrange the cut plastic pieces in your drawer to create sections that fit your needs. You can create equal-sized compartments or customize the sizes according to the items you plan to store. Experiment with different layouts until you find the configuration that works best for you.

Once you're satisfied with the arrangement, secure the dividers in place using adhesive materials. Apply glue or double-sided tape to the base of each plastic piece and attach them firmly to the bottom of the drawer. Make sure they are level and secure before moving on to the next step.

Now that your dividers are in place, you can further customize them to suit your style and needs. You can cover the bottom of the dividers with decorative paper or fabric to add a pop of color or pattern. Alternatively, you can leave them as they are for a clean and minimalist look.

Whether it's socks, underwear, stationery, or any other small items, these dividers will help you keep your drawer neat and organized. Enjoy the satisfaction of repurposing a single-use item into something both functional and stylish.

Remember, upcycling and repurposing are all about finding creative solutions to minimize waste. By transforming plastic takeout containers into drawer dividers, you're not only adding convenience to your daily life but also contributing to a more sustainable future. Happy crafting!.

Chapter 12: Upcycling Plastic Egg Cartons

- *Creating a seed starter tray*

This method is not only eco-friendly but also a great way to repurpose materials that would otherwise end up in the landfill. .

To make the seed starter tray, you will need a plastic egg carton, potting soil, seeds of your choice, a watering can or spray bottle, and a marker or labels for labeling the seeds. .

Start by obtaining a plastic egg carton. You can either save one from your own use or ask friends and neighbors if they have any spare cartons. .

Clean the egg carton thoroughly using soap and water. Make sure to remove any residue or food particles, as they may interfere with the germination of your seeds. Rinse the carton well and allow it to dry completely before proceeding to the next step. .

Once the egg carton is dry, it's time to prepare the soil. Fill each section of the carton with potting soil, leaving a small gap near the top for watering. Press down the soil gently to make it firm, ensuring that there are no air pockets. .

Next, decide which seeds you want to plant in each section. You can choose a variety of vegetables, herbs, or flowers, depending on your preferences. It's a good idea to label each section with the name of the seed to avoid confusion later on. .

Now, carefully plant the seeds in their respective sections, following the instructions on the seed packet for depth and spacing. Cover the seeds with a thin layer of soil and gently pat it down. .

After planting the seeds, it's important to water them properly. You can use a watering can with a fine spray or a spray bottle to mist the soil gently. Avoid overwatering, as it can lead to mold growth or root rot. .

Place the seed starter tray in a warm and well-lit area, but away from direct sunlight. You can cover the tray with a clear plastic dome or cling wrap to create a mini greenhouse effect, which will help retain moisture and promote germination. .

Monitor the seedlings regularly and keep the soil moist by watering when needed. As the seedlings grow, you may need to thin them out to prevent overcrowding. .

Once the seedlings have matured and are ready for transplanting, gently remove the individual sections from the egg carton. Plant them directly into pots or your garden, ensuring that they have enough space to grow. .

Remember to recycle the plastic egg carton once you have finished using it. You can reuse it for future seed starters or find other creative ways to repurpose it. .

By repurposing everyday items, you not only reduce waste but also contribute to a greener and more environmentally-friendly lifestyle.

- DIY Christmas ornaments

These ornaments are not only budget-friendly but also add a charming touch to your festive decorations.

Start by gathering some plastic egg cartons, preferably the ones that have individual slots for eggs. Cut the individual sections of the egg carton, making sure to trim off any excess or uneven edges. The aim is to have neat and uniform-looking sections.

Next, you can decide on the shape of your ornaments. For a classic ornament, choose a circular shape. Using a marker or pencil, trace circles onto the flat bottom part of the egg carton sections. Make as many circles as you desire, depending on the number of ornaments you want to create.

Once you have your circles marked, carefully cut them out using scissors. Take your time to ensure clean cuts and avoid any jagged edges. These circles will form the base of your ornaments.

Now it is time to unleash your creativity! You can paint the base of the ornaments using acrylic paints in various festive colors. Consider using metallic or glitter paints to add a touch of shimmer. Allow the paint to dry completely before moving on to the next step.

To add more visual interest to your ornaments, you can further embellish them with different materials. Here are a few suggestions:

1. Sequins and beads: Use a hot glue gun to attach sequins, beads, or rhinestones to the painted

surface of the ornaments. Create patterns or simply let your imagination guide you.

2. Ribbons and bows: Add a festive touch by gluing small ribbons or bows to the top of the ornaments. Choose colors that match your overall Christmas theme.

3. Faux greenery: Use small pieces of faux greenery, such as holly leaves or pine branches, to accentuate your ornaments. Secure them in place with a hot glue gun.

4. Personalized messages: If you have good penmanship, you can write short holiday messages or names on the ornaments using a gold or silver paint marker. This adds a personalized touch and makes the ornaments more meaningful.

Once you have decorated your ornaments to your satisfaction, it's time to add a hanger. Take a small piece of ribbon, twine, or decorative cord and create a loop, gluing the ends to the back of the ornament. This loop will serve as the hanger for your ornaments.

Allow the ornaments to dry completely and check for any loose or unsecured elements. If needed, add a final touch of clear glue or mod podge to secure any loose parts.

Now your upcycled plastic egg carton Christmas ornaments are ready to be displayed! Hang them on your Christmas tree, create a festive garland, or even use them as charming gift toppers. You can also encourage your friends and family to join in the fun by making their own DIY ornaments using this method.

Embrace the spirit of upcycling and repurposing by transforming everyday items into beautiful and unique Christmas ornaments. Plastic egg cartons, among other materials, provide endless possibilities for creativity and help reduce waste. Happy crafting and Merry Christmas!.

- Egg carton jewelry organizer

By repurposing plastic egg cartons, you can transform them into a useful and stylish storage solution for your jewelry collection. So, let's get started!.

First, gather all the materials you will need for this project. You will need a plastic egg carton, acrylic paint in your desired color, a foam paintbrush, fine-grit sandpaper, scissors, a ruler, a hot glue gun, and some decorative elements such as ribbon, beads, or sequins.

To begin, start by preparing your egg carton for upcycling. Remove any remaining eggs or eggshells from the carton and then thoroughly clean and dry it. If there are any labels or stickers on the carton, use warm soapy water to soak and remove them. Once cleaned, gently sand the surface of the carton using the fine-grit sandpaper. This will create a better surface for the paint to adhere to.

Next, it's time to paint your egg carton. Choose a color that matches your style and the rest of your décor. Using the foam paintbrush, apply a thin and even coat of acrylic paint to the entire exterior and interior of the carton. Allow the paint to dry completely before applying a second coat if needed. This will ensure a smooth and vibrant finish. Let the paint dry completely before moving on to the next step.

Once the paint has dried, it's time to transform the individual egg cups into compartments for your jewelry. Start by measuring the depth of the egg cups and determining how many compartments you would like. Using scissors, carefully cut the egg cups into separate sections, making sure the height of each compartment is uniform. Trim any rough edges or excess plastic.

Now, you can choose to further customize your jewelry organizer by adding decorative elements. You can attach a ribbon around the outside of the carton or glue beads, sequins, or other embellishments to the top and sides. Get creative and personalize it to your liking.

To make the jewelry organizer more functional, consider adding additional storage options. You can attach small hook screws to the inside of the egg cups to hang necklaces or bracelets. Alternatively, you can hot glue a piece of fabric inside each compartment to create a soft surface for delicate pieces. This will prevent them from getting scratched or tangled.

Once you have completed all the customization and functional additions, inspect your jewelry organizer for any loose or uneven elements. Make sure everything is securely attached and any excess glue is removed.

Now, you can proudly display your jewelry in a stylish and eco-friendly manner. Place the organizer on your vanity or hang it on the wall for easy access to your favorite pieces. This upcycling project not only repurposes a plastic egg carton but also helps you keep your jewelry organized and protected.

Remember, the key to successful upcycling and repurposing projects is to think creatively and look at everyday items from a different perspective. By transforming items that would otherwise be discarded, you can create functional and stylish creations while doing your part for the environment. Happy upcycling!.

Chapter 13: Repurposing Plastic Milk Jugs

- Plastic milk jug watering can

One of the interesting DIY projects that you can undertake involves repurposing plastic milk jugs into a watering can. This project offers a great way to upcycle your plastic milk jugs, adding a functional and stylish element to your garden. In this chapter, we will provide you with detailed instructions on how to create this DIY watering can.

To start, gather the following materials: a plastic milk jug, a sharp pair of scissors or a craft knife, a marker or pen, and a small nail or push pin. .

Begin by thoroughly cleaning and drying the plastic milk jug. Make sure to remove any labels or stickers, as these can interfere with the aesthetics of your finished watering can.

Next, using the marker or pen, draw a straight line across the center of the milk jug, from side to side. This line will serve as a guide for cutting the top portion of the jug.

Now, take your scissors or craft knife and carefully cut along the marked line. Be sure to use caution and keep your hands away from the blade to prevent any accidents.

Once the top portion of the milk jug has been removed, set it aside. This will be the section that you will use as the spout for your watering can.

Returning to the remaining lower portion of the milk jug, take the small nail or push pin and heat it up, either by holding it over a flame or using a heated tool. Once the nail is heated, carefully poke several small holes in the bottom of the jug. These holes will allow water to flow out when you use the watering can.

After creating the holes, place the top portion of the milk jug, which you had set aside, back onto the lower portion. Ensure that it fits securely and aligns with the spout section.

Congratulations! You have successfully repurposed your plastic milk jug into a functional watering can. Now, you can use this DIY creation to effortlessly hydrate your plants and keep them thriving.

By upcycling everyday items, such as plastic shower curtains, plastic laundry detergent bottles, plastic shampoo bottles, plastic lotion bottles, paper towel rolls, toilet paper rolls, plastic grocery bags, plastic food packaging, plastic clamshell containers, plastic takeout containers, plastic egg cartons, plastic soda bottles, wine corks, wine bottles, glass jars, glass bottles, tin cans, aluminum cans, and paper bags, you can not only reduce waste but also add a unique touch to your living space. Let your creativity flow and enjoy the process of transforming these items into functional and stylish creations.

- DIY bird feeder

This project is not only practical, but also environmentally friendly, as it gives a second life to materials that would otherwise end up in the landfill.

To begin, gather the following materials: a plastic milk jug, a sharp utility knife, a marker or pen, a metal coat hanger or wire, birdseed, and a pair of pliers. .

First, thoroughly clean the plastic milk jug, ensuring that it is free from any residue or lingering odors. Once clean, allow it to dry completely before proceeding with the project.

Once the milk jug is dry, you can start by marking and cutting an opening for the birds to access the birdseed. Use the marker or pen to draw a rectangular or circular shape on the front or side of the milk jug, leaving enough space for the birds to comfortably access the birdseed. Remember to keep the opening size proportional to the size of the birds you wish to attract.

Next, carefully cut out the marked opening using a sharp utility knife. Take your time during this step to ensure a clean and precise cut. Be mindful of your fingers and use caution when handling the knife.

After the opening is cut, use the pliers to bend the sharp edges inward to provide a safer surface for the birds to perch on. Smooth out any rough or jagged edges using the pliers to prevent any potential harm to the birds or yourself.

Now it's time to create a way to hang the bird feeder. Take the metal coat hanger or wire and straighten it out, then bend one end into a hook shape. Insert the hook end into the milk jug's opening, ensuring it is securely positioned. If you prefer, you can also use a sturdy string or rope instead of a coat hanger to hang the bird feeder.

Fill the bottom portion of the milk jug with birdseed, leaving enough room for the birds to comfortably access the seeds through the opening. Make sure to choose a birdseed suitable for the type of birds you want to attract, as different birds have different preferences.

Hang the bird feeder in a location where it is easily visible for you to enjoy watching the visiting birds. Ideally, place it in a quiet area away from predators, such as cats or squirrels, but also near a tree or bush for the birds to take cover if needed.

Remember to regularly clean and refill the bird feeder to ensure a healthy and inviting environment for the birds. Clean out any leftover seeds and debris, and refill with fresh birdseed as necessary.

Enjoy the serene beauty of nature as you watch the birds flock to your upcycled creation.

- Milk jug herb garden

This project is a practical and innovative way to make use of plastic milk jugs, turning them into functional and aesthetically pleasing planters for growing herbs. .

To start, gather your materials. You will need several clean and empty plastic milk jugs, a utility knife or scissors, potting soil, herbs of your choice, and water. .

Begin by cleaning and rinsing the milk jugs thoroughly to remove any residue. Once they are dry, use a utility knife or scissors to carefully cut out the top portion of each milk jug. Leave about two-thirds of the jug intact, creating a sturdy base for your herb garden.

Next, make small drainage holes on the bottom of the milk jugs to prevent water from accumulating and causing root rot. Use a sharp knife or a heated needle to carefully poke a few holes in the bottom of each jug. .

Now it's time to prepare the herbs for planting. Choose your desired herbs based on your preferences and climate. Popular choices for herb gardens include basil, mint, rosemary, thyme, and parsley. Purchase young herb plants from a nursery or start your own from seeds.

Fill the bottom one-third of each milk jug with potting soil. Gently remove the herb plants from their containers and loosen the roots. Place one or two herb plants into each milk jug, ensuring they have enough space to grow. Add more potting soil around the plants, filling the jugs almost to the rim.

Water the newly planted herbs gently, ensuring the soil is moist but not overly saturated. Most herbs thrive in direct sunlight for at least six hours a day.

Remember to water your herb garden regularly to keep the soil evenly moist. Check the soil with your finger to determine if it's dry before watering. Avoid overwatering, as it can lead to root rot.

As your herb garden grows, monitor the plants for any signs of pests or diseases. Remove any dead leaves or prune the herbs when necessary to promote healthy growth. Harvest the herbs as needed for use in your cooking or to enjoy their aromatic scents.

By repurposing plastic milk jugs into a DIY herb garden, you not only create a functional and sustainable planter but also contribute to reducing waste and promoting green living. This project is a great way to showcase your creativity while enjoying the benefits of fresh herbs at your fingertips.

Chapter 14: Upcycling Plastic Soda Bottles

- Crafting a piggy bank

Plastic soda bottles are often found in abundance in households and can be easily repurposed into various DIY creations. In this part of Chapter 14, we will guide you in crafting a unique piggy bank using plastic soda bottles. Let's delve into the step-by-step process of upcycling and repurposing these bottles into a functional and stylish creation.

To start, gather the following materials:

- Plastic soda bottles (preferably with a clear or translucent body, as it allows for easy visibility of the saved coins).

- Craft knife or scissors.

- Sandpaper.

- Acrylic paint or spray paint in your preferred color(s).

- Paintbrushes.

- Marker or pen.

- Hot glue gun or strong adhesive.

Once you have assembled the required materials, follow these instructions to create your own piggy bank:

1. Preparation: Begin by thoroughly cleaning the plastic soda bottles. Remove any labels, and if required, peel off the top portion to create an open mouth for depositing coins.

2. Design: Once the bottles are clean, you can unleash your creativity to design the appearance of your piggy bank. Consider using a marker or pen to outline the desired shape and features such as eyes, nose, and mouth onto the bottle's surface. This will

help you achieve a uniform and attractive appearance.

3. Cutting: Carefully cut along the marked lines on the plastic soda bottles using a craft knife or scissors. Make sure to follow the lines precisely to achieve the desired shape. This step might require adult supervision, especially if children are involved in the crafting process.

4. Smoothing edges: After cutting the bottles, use sandpaper to gently smoothen any rough edges. This will give your piggy bank a polished and safe finish.

5. Painting: Apply acrylic paint or spray paint in your chosen colors to the outer surface of the soda bottles. Allow the paint to dry completely before moving on to the next step. You can apply multiple coats to achieve a vibrant and opaque finish.

6. Assembly: Once the paint has dried, it's time to assemble your piggy bank. Use a hot glue gun or a strong adhesive to secure the various parts of the

soda bottles together. Ensure that all edges and joints are firmly glued to avoid any accidental spills of the saved coins.

7. Coin slot: Cut a small rectangular slot on the top portion of your piggy bank to insert the coins. This slot can be located on the bottle or at the piggy bank's head, depending on your creative preference.

8. Finishing touches: Complete your piggy bank by adding final details such as ears, a curly tail (made using paper or other suitable materials), or any other adornments to make it truly unique and personal. Let your imagination run wild!.

There you have it – a beautifully upcycled piggy bank crafted from plastic soda bottles. Display your creation proudly and start saving money in an eco-friendly and creative way. Remember to encourage others to replicate this DIY project and spread the joy of upcycling everyday items.

Revisit Chapter 14 for countless other creative ideas on upcycling and repurposing various items.

Enjoy the process of transforming mundane materials into extraordinary pieces of art while reducing waste and contributing to a more sustainable world. Happy crafting!.

- DIY vertical garden

This guide will provide you with a detailed and comprehensive explanation to assist you in creating your very own vertical garden utilizing these readily available materials.

Plastic soda bottles can be easily repurposed into plant containers for vertical gardens. Start by cutting the bottle in half, ensuring that the bottom portion is larger than the top. Next, make holes in the bottle cap to allow for watering and drainage. Fill the bottom half with potting soil and add your desired plants. Fit the top half of the bottle over the plant-filled section, securing it tightly. Hang the bottle vertically and watch as your plants grow beautifully.

Cut the curtain into smaller pieces, each large enough to hold a plant. Punch holes into the plastic to allow for water drainage. Attach these pieces to a wall or fence using nails, hooks, or zip ties. Fill each pocket with soil and plant your chosen greenery. The plastic shower curtains will serve as a protective barrier against soil erosion and water run-off.

Cut these bottles in half and discard the bottom portion. Make sure to clean the bottles thoroughly to remove any residue. Next, create drainage holes at the bottom of the bottle. Fill the top section with soil and plant your desired herbs, flowers, or succulents. Attach the bottles vertically to a wall or fence, allowing the plants to cascade downwards.

Paper towel and toilet paper rolls are great for starting plant seedlings before transferring them to your vertical garden. Fill these rolls with potting soil and plant your seeds. Place the rolls in a tray or container and keep them in a warm, well-lit area until the seeds germinate. Once the seedlings are ready, carefully remove the rolls and transplant them into your vertical garden.

Plastic grocery bags, food packaging, clamshell containers, takeout containers, egg cartons, and milk jugs can all be utilized for creating self-watering planters in your vertical garden. Cut the containers in half, ensuring that the bottom half can hold water. Create a small hole near the top of the container, ensuring it is large enough for water to be slowly absorbed by the soil. Fill the bottom half of the container with water, and then place the top half on top, filled with soil and your chosen plants. The plants will absorb water through the hole by capillary action, providing them with a constant supply of moisture.

Wine corks, wine bottles, glass jars, and glass bottles can add a touch of elegance to your vertical garden. Use wine corks to craft small plant holders by creating holes to insert the plants. Clean and remove labels from wine bottles, jars, and bottles before using them as decorative plant containers. Hang these glass containers vertically, ensuring they are securely fastened, and fill them with soil and plants.

Clean and remove labels from these cans before using them. Attach the can vertically to a wall or fence. Make drainage holes at the bottom of the can and fill it with soil and plants. These containers can be easily customized by painting or decorating them to match the aesthetic of your vertical garden.

Lastly, consider using paper bags for temporary planting solutions in your vertical garden. Fold the bags into a sturdy shape, fill them with soil, and plant your desired greenery. These bags can be easily replaced or repurposed when necessary.

Let your imagination and creativity run wild as you transform these items into functional and aesthetically pleasing plant holders in your vertical garden.

- Plastic bottle broom

Plastic soda bottles are a common item found in households, and they can be easily upcycled and repurposed into various functional and stylish creations. This project is not only simple and cost-effective but also environmentally friendly as it diverts plastic bottles from going into landfills.

First, gather the materials you will need for this project. You will need a plastic soda bottle, a sturdy stick or handle, a sharp knife or scissors, a marker, a drill with a 1/8 inch drill bit, a sturdy wire or twine, and sandpaper.

Start by preparing the plastic soda bottle. Rinse it out thoroughly with water to remove any residue. Once it is clean and dry, use a marker to mark a line around the bottle, approximately two-thirds of the way up from the bottom. This line will act as a guide for cutting.

Next, carefully cut the bottle along the marked line using a sharp knife or scissors. Make sure to follow the line accurately to ensure a clean cut. Take your time and exercise caution to avoid any injuries.

After cutting the bottle, discard the top section as it will not be needed for this project. You will be left with the bottom section of the bottle, which will form the bristles of the broom.

Now it's time to create holes in the bottle for attaching the bristles to the stick or handle. Use a drill with a 1/8 inch drill bit to make evenly spaced holes around the outer edge of the bottle's bottom section. These holes will be used to secure the bristles to the stick or handle.

Once the holes are drilled, take your sandpaper and smooth out any rough edges around the cut and drilled areas. This will ensure that the broom is safe to use and doesn't cause any harm.

Now, onto attaching the bristles to the stick or handle. Take a sturdy wire or twine and thread it through one of the holes in the bottle's bottom section. Securely tie the wire or twine to the stick or handle. Repeat this step for each hole, making sure to pull the wire or twine tightly so that the bristles are held firmly.

Once all the bristles are attached, give the broom a few test sweeps to ensure that the bristles are securely held in place and the broom is functioning properly.

This DIY project not only helps to reduce waste but also provides a useful tool for household cleaning.

Remember, the possibilities for upcycling and repurposing everyday items are endless. Be creative and let your imagination run wild. With just a little effort and some simple materials, you can transform common household items into functional and stylish creations. Happy crafting!.

Chapter 15: Repurposing Wine Corks

- Creating a corkboard

This step-by-step guide will provide you with clear instructions and expert tips to help you transform ordinary wine corks into a functional and stylish corkboard. .

To begin, gather all the materials you will need for this project. Since the focus of this chapter is on repurposing wine corks, ensure you have a significant number of wine corks available. This will depend on the size of the corkboard you wish to create. Additionally, you will need a sturdy backing material for your corkboard. Consider using materials such as plywood or corkboard sheets. Other essential materials include a hot glue gun, a measuring tape, a ruler, a pencil, and a utility knife or scissors for cutting the backing material if necessary.

Start by measuring and marking the desired dimensions for your corkboard on the backing material. This will determine the size of the finished product. Use a ruler and a pencil to ensure accuracy. Once you have marked the dimensions, cut the backing material accordingly. If you are using plywood, you may need to use a utility knife or a saw for this step.

Next, arrange the wine corks on the prepared backing material in your desired pattern. This is where your creativity can truly shine. You can create a uniform pattern, a random arrangement, or even use different colored corks for a more vibrant look. Take your time to find the arrangement that pleases you the most.

Now it's time to attach the wine corks to the backing material. Using a hot glue gun, apply a generous amount of glue to the bottom of each cork and press firmly onto the backing material. Hold the cork in place for a few seconds to allow the glue to set. Repeat this step until all the wine corks are securely glued in place.

Once the glue has dried completely, your corkboard is ready to be displayed. Hang it on a wall using appropriate hooks or place it on a tabletop by using a stand or an easel. This corkboard can serve as a practical and decorative item in your home or office, providing you with a convenient place to pin notes, photographs, or other important reminders.

By repurposing materials that might have otherwise been discarded, you are contributing to a more sustainable lifestyle.

This DIY project allows you to showcase your creativity while also playing a part in reducing environmental impact. Enjoy the process and take pride in your upcycled creation!.

- *Wine cork keychain or necklace*

Upcycling and repurposing everyday items is not only a sustainable practice but a creative way to transform them into functional and stylish creations.

To start this project, gather the following materials: wine corks, small eye screws or screw eyes, jump rings, lobster clasps, a chain or cord, pliers, and an awl or small drill.

First, examine your wine corks and decide which ones you will use for your keychain or necklace. Consider the length, thickness, and condition of the corks. You may choose to use corks from different wine bottles, depending on the variation you desire.

Once you have selected your wine corks, prepare them for assembly. Using the awl or small drill, carefully create a small hole at the top center of each cork. This will be where you will attach the screw eyes later on. Be cautious while creating the holes to prevent any injuries.

Now, insert the screw eyes into the holes you just created in the corks. You may need to use pliers to screw them in securely. Ensure that the screw eyes are firmly attached to prevent them from coming loose later on.

After attaching the screw eyes, it's time to connect the corks together to create the keychain or necklace. Open a jump ring using pliers and slide it through the screw eye of one cork. Then, add another wine cork to the jump ring, connecting them together. Continue this process until all your desired corks are connected.

Once all the corks are securely linked, you can now attach the lobster clasp to one end of the chain or cord using another jump ring. On the other end of the chain or cord, attach a jump ring without the lobster clasp. These will serve as the closures for your keychain or necklace.

Now, your DIY creation is ready to be enjoyed and showcased!.

Remember, this is just one creative way to repurpose wine corks. With your imagination and DIY skills, you can experiment with different designs, colors, and materials to make unique keychains or necklaces that reflect your personal style.

By upcycling these everyday items, you not only give them a new life but also contribute to a more sustainable lifestyle.

- DIY stamp for crafts

These versatile little items can be transformed into unique DIY stamps for crafts that you can easily make at home. So, let's get started!.

To create a DIY stamp using wine corks, you will need a few materials and tools. Here's a list of what you'll need:

1. Wine corks: Start collecting wine corks from your favorite bottles. The more you have, the more stamping possibilities you'll have.

2. Sharp knife or craft scissors: You'll need a tool to cut the design into the cork. A sharp knife or craft scissors will work perfectly for this purpose.

3. Craft paint: Choose acrylic craft paint in various colors, depending on your design preferences.

4. Paintbrush: Get a small paintbrush that can be easily maneuvered to apply paint to the stamps.

5. Paper or cardstock: You'll need a surface to test your stamps and create your stamped designs. Paper or cardstock in different colors can be used for this.

Now that you have all the required materials, let's move on to the step-by-step process of creating your DIY stamp using wine corks:

1. Clean and dry the wine corks: Before starting, make sure your wine corks are clean and dry. This

will ensure better adherence of paint and avoid any unwanted residue on your stamped designs.

2. Choose your design: Think about what design you want to create using the stamp. It can be a simple geometric shape, a flower, an animal, or anything that inspires you. The possibilities are endless!.

3. Cut the design: Take a wine cork and using a sharp knife or craft scissors, carefully cut the desired design into one end of the cork. Make sure to go deep enough to create a clear stamp, but be cautious not to cut yourself.

4. Apply paint to the stamp: Dip your paintbrush into the craft paint and carefully apply a thin, even layer to the cut surface of the cork. Make sure not to overload the stamp with paint to avoid smudging.

5. Test the stamp: Press the painted stamp onto a piece of paper or cardstock to test the design. If you're happy with the result, you're ready to start stamping on your desired project.

6. Stamp away: Now that your DIY stamp is ready, you can start stamping on various surfaces. Consider using it on paper crafts, fabric, or even walls for a unique touch.

Remember to clean your stamp after each use to prevent colors from mixing. You can either wash it with warm water and mild soap or simply wipe it clean with a damp cloth.

By repurposing wine corks into DIY stamps, you not only save them from ending up in landfills but also give them a new purpose and unleash your creativity. So, start gathering those wine corks and let your imagination run wild with these personalized stamps for your crafts. Happy stamping!.

Chapter 16: Upcycling Wine Bottles

- *Making a decorative candle holder*

This DIY project is not only fun and creative but also a great way to give new life to old wine bottles.

To make a decorative candle holder from a wine bottle, you will need a few materials and tools. Firstly, gather the following items:

1. Wine bottle.
2. Craft knife or glass cutter.
3. Sandpaper or emery cloth.
4. Acetone or rubbing alcohol.
5. Paintbrush.

6. Acrylic paint in your preferred color(s).

7. Decorative items such as ribbons, charms, or beads.

8. Mod Podge or clear glue.

9. Tealight candle or LED tea light.

Let's begin by preparing the wine bottle for upcycling. Remove any labels or stickers on the bottle by soaking it in warm, soapy water. If there is any residue left, use acetone or rubbing alcohol to clean the surface thoroughly.

Next, the bottle needs to be cut to create an opening for the candle. There are a few methods you can use to cut the wine bottle safely. One option is using a craft knife or glass cutter to score a line around the bottle, being careful to apply consistent pressure. Once the line is scored, apply hot and cold water alternately to the scored area until the bottle separates. Alternatively, you can use a specialized bottle-cutting tool for a more precise cut.

After the bottle has been cut, use sandpaper or emery cloth to smooth the edges, making sure they are free from any sharp or rough areas. Safety should always be a priority when handling glass, so take your time with this step.

Now it's time to unleash your creativity! Take your paintbrush and apply acrylic paint to the outside of the bottle. Choose colors that match your decor or go for a unique and eye-catching design. Apply multiple coats if needed, allowing each layer to dry before moving on to the next.

Once the paint is dry, it's time to add some decorative touches. Wrap ribbons or twine around the neck of the bottle, or attach charms or beads for added charm. Secure these embellishments with Mod Podge or clear glue, allowing them to dry completely.

Finally, place a tealight candle or LED tea light inside the bottle, and your upcycled wine bottle candle holder is ready to light up your space. Remember to never leave candles unattended and ensure the flame is extinguished before leaving the room.

By upcycling wine bottles into decorative candle holders, you not only create a unique piece of decor but also reduce waste and contribute to a more sustainable lifestyle. The possibilities for upcycling and repurposing everyday items are endless, offering a chance to be environmentally conscious while showcasing your creativity. Experiment with different materials and techniques, and have fun transforming ordinary objects into extraordinary works of art.

- *Wine bottle chandelier*

This project requires patience, attention to detail, and some basic crafting skills.

Step 1: Gather Materials.

To begin this project, you will need the following materials:

- Approximately 8-10 empty wine bottles (The number can vary depending on the size and design of your chandelier).

- Wire cutters.

- Pliers.

- Ceiling fixture kit with sockets and wiring.

- Chain or rope for hanging the chandelier.

- Light bulbs (LED bulbs are preferable for energy efficiency).

- Optional: Decorative elements such as beads or crystals for embellishments.

Step 2: Prepare the Wine Bottles.

Start by removing any labels on the bottles by soaking them in warm soapy water or using a label remover product. Once the labels are removed, thoroughly clean and dry the bottles. It's critical to ensure that the bottles are completely dry to prevent any electrical hazards.

Next, use wire cutters to carefully remove the bottom portion of each wine bottle. This step will create an opening through which the light will shine. Be careful while cutting to avoid any sharp edges. You can then use a file or sandpaper to smoothen the cut edges, making them safer to handle.

Step 3: Wiring the Wine Bottles.

Now that your wine bottles are prepared, it's time to wire them for the chandelier. Begin by threading the wire from the ceiling fixture kit through the mouth of one of the wine bottles, ensuring it is securely held in place. You can use pliers to twist the wire and create a loop at the top for hanging.

Continue this process for all the wine bottles that you plan to include in your chandelier design. For a beautiful arrangement, consider mixing and matching wine bottle colors and shapes. Experiment with different combinations until you achieve the desired look.

Step 4: Assembling the Chandelier.

Once all the wine bottles are wired, it's time to assemble your chandelier. Begin by attaching the wired wine bottles to the ceiling fixture kit, ensuring they are evenly spaced and balanced. This step requires some creativity and patience to achieve a visually appealing result.

Next, connect the wiring from the ceiling fixture kit to a power source. If you're unfamiliar with electrical work, it's recommended to consult an electrician or seek assistance from a knowledgeable friend.

Step 5: Adding the Finishing Touches.

You can attach these elements to the bottles or drape them along the chain or rope used for hanging. This step is entirely optional and can be tailored to your personal style and preferences.

Step 6: Hanging the Chandelier.

Use strong chain or rope to hang the chandelier from the hook, ensuring it is level and balanced.

Remember to exercise caution and prioritize safety throughout the entire process. If you encounter any difficulties, don't hesitate to seek assistance or guidance from knowledgeable individuals.

Upcycling and repurposing everyday items like wine bottles not only contribute to a more sustainable lifestyle but also allow you to unleash your creativity and add a personal touch to your decor. Enjoy the process and happy crafting!.

- DIY vase from wine bottles

In this chapter, we will explore the art of upcycling and repurposing everyday items, specifically focusing on transforming wine bottles into unique DIY vases. By giving a new life to these wine bottles, we can create functional and stylish home decor pieces that not only reduce waste but also add charm and character to our living spaces.

To start this project, you will require the following materials:

- Wine bottles (various sizes and shapes).

- Protective gloves and eyewear.

- Wine bottle cutter or a glass cutter.

- Water source.

- Sandpaper (various grits).

- Acetone or nail polish remover.

- Paintbrushes.

- Acrylic paint or spray paint.

- Stencils or masking tape (optional).

- Varnish or clear coat (optional).

- Decorative items like twine, beads, or ribbons (optional).

- Flowers or greenery for displaying in the finished vase.

1. Preparation: Safety First!.

Before embarking on this project, ensure you have taken all necessary safety precautions. Wear protective gloves and eyewear throughout the entire process to avoid any injuries while handling glass.

2. Selecting Wine Bottles:

Choose wine bottles of different sizes, shapes, and colors to create an eclectic mix of vases. Whether you prefer Bordeaux bottles or elegant champagne bottles, selecting a variety will allow for a visually appealing display.

3. Bottle Cutting:

Use a wine bottle cutter or a glass cutter to score the desired cutting line around the bottle. Follow the instructions provided by the manufacturer to ensure proper usage of the cutting tool. After scoring the glass, carefully apply pressure to create a clean break. You may need to practice a few times to achieve the desired results.

4. Smoothing the Edges:

Once the bottle is cut, the edges might be rough. To smoothen them, use sandpaper of various grits to gradually polish the edges. Start with a coarse-grit sandpaper and gradually work your way to a finer grit. Be sure to sand both the outer and inner edges to achieve a polished finish.

5. Removing Labels:

To remove any labels or adhesive residue from the wine bottle, soak it in warm soapy water for a few hours. Then, use a scraper or rubbing alcohol to gently scrub off any remaining residue. If needed, acetone or nail polish remover can be used to remove stubborn glue.

6. Painting and Decorating:

Now it's time to unleash your creativity! Decide on the colors and patterns you wish to use on your DIY vase. Acrylic paint or spray paint works well for this purpose. You can also use stencils or masking tape to create unique designs. Remember to paint the outside of the bottle only, leaving the inside clear for displaying flowers or greenery later.

7. Sealing (Optional):

To protect the painted surface and add a glossy finish, you can apply varnish or a clear coat according to the instructions on the product. This step is optional but will provide extra durability and longevity to your vase.

8. Adding Decorative Touches (Optional):

For additional charm and personalization, you can tie twine, beads, or ribbons around the neck of the bottle. These decorative elements will enhance the overall aesthetic appeal of the finished DIY vase.

9. Displaying Your DIY Vase:

Finally, place your vases on a shelf, windowsill, or any desired spot in your home. Fill them with fresh flowers or greenery to bring a touch of nature indoors. You can change the arrangements according to the season or your preferences, allowing for a constantly evolving display.

By following these steps, you can upcycle and repurpose wine bottles into beautiful DIY vases. This creative project not only promotes sustainability but also showcases your artistic skills. Enjoy the process and revel in the unique creations you can make with simple, everyday items.

Chapter 17: Repurposing Glass Jars

- Creating storage containers

Glass jars are versatile, readily available, and can be transformed into stylish containers for various purposes, from organizing small items to elegantly displaying decorative pieces.

To begin, gather a collection of glass jars in different shapes and sizes. These can be repurposed jars from food products, such as jam, salsa, or pickles, or even empty candle jars. Ensure that the jars are thoroughly cleaned and free of any residual odors or debris.

One practical and visually appealing option for repurposing glass jars is to create a tiered storage system. This can be accomplished by securely attaching the lids of multiple jars together in a stacked formation using strong adhesive or a hot glue gun. This tiered system allows for efficient storage of small items, such as craft supplies, buttons, or jewelry, while also serving as a decorative display piece for your shelves or counter.

For a more decorative purpose, consider transforming glass jars into beautiful terrariums or miniature gardens. Begin by layering the bottom of the jar with small stones or gravel for drainage. Add a layer of activated charcoal to prevent any odors or mold growth. Then, fill the jar with soil and carefully plant your chosen succulents, moss, or other small plants. Finally, adorn the lid or neck of the jar with decorative elements such as ribbons, twine, or small ornaments.

To create an organized storage solution for your kitchen or pantry, repurpose glass jars with airtight lids as food containers. Remove the labels and ensure that the jars are completely clean and dry. Fill them with ingredients such as rice, pasta, or lentils, and label each jar for easy identification. The transparent glass adds a touch of elegance and allows you to quickly see the contents of each jar, making your kitchen more organized and visually appealing.

For a charming and eco-friendly idea, upcycle glass jars into lanterns or candle holders. Begin by removing the lids and any labels, and thoroughly clean the jars. Wrap the neck of the jar with twine or ribbon and secure it with hot glue. Insert a tea light candle or a battery-operated votive into the jar, and your homemade lantern is ready to bring a warm and cozy glow to your outdoor space or indoor ambiance.

Whether you create tiered storage systems, terrariums, food containers, or lanterns, glass jars are a versatile medium with great potential for DIY projects. Tap into your creativity, explore different ideas, and let your imagination guide you as you transform these everyday items into unique and useful creations. Enjoy the process and remember to always prioritize safety when working with glass and other materials!.

- Crafting a homemade snow globe

In this chapter, we will explore the creative potential of repurposing glass jars to make a unique and enchanting homemade snow globe. Glass jars are easily accessible and can be found in most households, making them a perfect material to repurpose into a snow globe.

To begin, gather your materials. You will need a glass jar with a tight-fitting lid, distilled water, glycerin or baby oil, glitter or faux snow, a waterproof adhesive, a small figurine or object, and optional decorative elements like ribbon or miniature ornaments.

First, ensure that your glass jar is clean and dry. Any residue or dirt will affect the aesthetics of the snow globe. You can wash it with soap and warm water, or use a glass cleaning solution for a more thorough cleaning.

Next, select a small figurine or object that will serve as the centerpiece of your snow globe. It should be waterproof and durable enough to withstand being submerged in water. Ideas for objects can range from small plastic toys to decorative figurines or even small plants like moss or air plants.

Using a waterproof adhesive, carefully glue the object to the inside of the lid of the glass jar. Allow the adhesive to fully dry and cure according to the manufacturer's instructions. This step ensures that your object stays securely in place when the snow globe is shaken.

Once the adhesive has dried, fill the glass jar with distilled water, leaving some space at the top for the displacement caused by the object and glitter. Add a few drops of glycerin or baby oil to the water. This helps slow down the falling of the glitter or faux snow, creating a more mesmerizing snowstorm effect.

Now it's time to add the magical snow-like effect! Sprinkle glitter or faux snow into the water, using a quantity that suits your preference.

Experiment with different colors or sizes of glitter for a more personalized touch. Remember, less is often more with glitter, as excessive amounts can overwhelm the snow globe.

Carefully screw the lid back onto the glass jar, ensuring a tight and secure fit. Test the seal by gently shaking the snow globe; there should be no leaks or seepage of water. If necessary, seal any gaps with a waterproof adhesive.

Once your snow globe is fully assembled, you can further customize it with decorative elements. Tie a ribbon around the rim of the jar, add miniature ornaments to the lid, or attach a small tag with a personalized message. These decorative touches add an extra layer of charm to your homemade snow globe.

Now, ready to see your creation come to life? Give the snow globe a gentle shake, and watch as the glitter or faux snow dances and swirls around your centerpiece. Display your unique snow globe on a shelf, mantelpiece, or as a thoughtful homemade gift for friends and loved ones.

With just a few simple steps, you can breathe new life into discarded jars and create whimsical snow globes that will bring joy and wonder to any space. Happy crafting!.

- *Glass jar lanterns*

By repurposing glass jars, you not only contribute to the reduction of waste but also add a charming and whimsical element to your DIY projects.

1. Glass jars (various shapes and sizes): The key to creating visually appealing lanterns is the diversity of the glass jars you choose. Opt for vintage mason jars, jam jars, or even old sauce jars. Different sizes will add depth and variation to your lanterns.

2. Glue or Mod Podge: Ensuring a secure bond between your decorative elements and the glass surface of the jar is crucial. You can choose to use a strong adhesive glue or Mod Podge, a versatile sealer, glue, and finisher.

3. Paint or spray paint: If you prefer a personalized touch or want to match your lanterns to a specific color scheme, consider using paint or spray paint. Choose outdoor-friendly options if you plan to display your lanterns outdoors.

4. Decorative elements: The decoration possibilities are endless. Choose from a variety of materials such as seashells, pebbles, twigs, beads, ribbons, or even colorful tissue paper.

1. Prepare the glass jars: Start by thoroughly cleaning and drying the glass jars. Remove any labels or sticky residue using warm soapy water or a gentle adhesive remover.

2. Paint the jar (optional): If you want to add a pop of color or create a cohesive look, consider painting the exterior of your glass jars. Make sure to apply multiple thin coats for a smooth and even finish. Allow the paint to dry completely before proceeding.

3. Apply decorative elements: Once the paint has dried (if you chose to paint the jars), it's time to add your chosen decorative elements. Using glue or Mod Podge, carefully attach the items to the jars. Arrange them in a way that is visually pleasing to you.

4. Add lighting: To transform your glass jar into a lantern, you'll need to choose a lighting option. Tea lights, LED lights, or even battery-operated fairy lights work well for this purpose. For safety reasons, opt for flameless options.

5. Place them on tabletops, along staircases, or hang them from outdoor trees using twine or wire.

They also make fantastic and thoughtful gifts for friends and loved ones. Whether it's for birthdays, housewarmings, or special occasions, you can personalize each lantern based on the recipient's taste and preferences.

By embracing your artistic side and utilizing various decorative elements, you can transform plain jars into enchanting and stylish decor pieces.

Chapter 18: Upcycling Glass Bottles

- DIY bottle lamps

Glass bottles come in various shapes and sizes, making them excellent materials for crafting unique and personalized lamps. In this chapter, we will dive into the process of upcycling glass bottles to create one-of-a-kind bottle lamps to add style and ambiance to your living space.

You can use old wine bottles, glass jars, or any other glass containers with interesting shapes or colors. Make sure to clean the bottles thoroughly and remove any labels or adhesive residue before you start the transformation process.

Start by preparing the materials you'll need for this project. You will require a glass-cutting tool, such as a glass cutter or glass drill bit, to make a hole in the bottom of the bottle for electrical wiring. Additionally, gather a lamp kit, which typically includes a socket, cord, plug, and a switch. You can easily find lamp kits at your local hardware store or online.

Once you have your materials ready, it's time to carefully cut a hole in the bottom of the glass bottle. Follow the instructions provided with your glass-cutting tool to ensure safety and accuracy. Remember to wear protective gloves and eyewear during this step to prevent any injuries.

Next, assemble the lamp kit according to the manufacturer's instructions. Thread the cord through the hole in the bottle, leaving enough length on the inside to connect it to the socket. Attach the socket and the plug to the respective ends of the cord, making sure to secure them tightly. If desired, you can also add a switch to the cord for convenient operation.

Now that the electrical aspect is taken care of, it's time to add the finishing touches to your DIY bottle lamp. Choose a bulb that matches the socket specifications and screw it into place. You can opt for traditional incandescent bulbs or experiment with energy-efficient LED bulbs for a longer-lasting and environmentally friendly choice.

To enhance the aesthetic appeal of your bottle lamp, you can decorate the bottle using various techniques. Consider painting the glass or applying adhesive decals or stickers to create interesting patterns or designs. You can also play with different lampshade options to diffuse the light and add an extra layer of style. Explore fabric, paper, or even repurposed materials such as woven baskets or metal mesh to craft your unique lampshade.

Finally, find the perfect spot to display your newly created DIY bottle lamp. Whether it's a corner table, a shelf, or a bedside stand, the warm glow emitted by the lamp will create a cozy and inviting atmosphere wherever it's placed. Experiment with pairing multiple bottle lamps together to form a visually captivating arrangement.

Get inspired by the various shapes and sizes of glass bottles available and let your imagination run wild to create extraordinary lighting pieces that showcase your personal style and contribute to a more eco-friendly lifestyle.

- Creating a bottle vase or centerpiece

In this chapter, we'll explore the art of upcycling glass bottles to create stunning vases or centerpieces that will add a touch of elegance to any space. The upcycling process not only helps reduce waste but also allows us to transform everyday items into functional and stylish creations. Get ready to unleash your creativity and bring new life to those old glass bottles!.

Before we dive into the upcycling techniques, let's gather the necessary materials to embark on this project. You'll need the following items:

1. Glass Bottles: Collect various glass bottles in different shapes and sizes. Wine bottles, perfume

bottles, and jars are great options to work with. You can either source them from your own collection or scout local thrift stores, yard sales, or recycling centers.

Now, let's move on to the upcycling process itself. Here's a step-by-step guide to help you turn those glass bottles into unique vases or centerpieces:

Step 1: Cleaning the Bottles.

Ensure that the glass bottles you've collected are thoroughly cleaned and free from any residual liquids. Soak them in warm soapy water, and gently scrub away any labels or adhesive residue. Rinse them well and let them dry completely before proceeding to the next step.

Step 2: Removing Labels (Optional).

If any labels persist on the bottles, you can use various methods to remove them. Soaking the bottles in warm water mixed with dish soap can help loosen the adhesive. Alternatively, you can apply a mixture of equal parts baking soda and oil (such as coconut or olive oil) onto the labels and allow it to sit for a few minutes. Then, scrub with a sponge or scrape off the labels using a razor blade or a plastic scraper. Rinse the bottles thoroughly to remove any residue from the oil or baking soda.

Step 3: Applying Paint or Decorative Technique.

Now comes the fun part! Decide on the design or color scheme you want for your bottle vase or centerpiece. You can go for a classic look by painting the bottles with a single color or experiment with various decorative techniques such as etching, decoupage, or stencil art. Use acrylic or glass-specific paint for best results. Apply multiple coats as necessary and follow the instructions on the paint bottle for drying times between coats.

Step 4: Embellishing the Bottles (Optional).

To add an extra touch of creativity and personalization, consider embellishing the bottles with various materials. You can use twine, ribbons, lace, beads, or even create a mosaic pattern using broken glass or ceramic pieces. Secure these embellishments in place with hot glue or an appropriate adhesive.

Step 5: Finishing Touches with Florals or Decorative Fillers.

Finally, it's time to fill your upcycled bottle vase or centerpiece. You can choose to use fresh flowers if you plan on changing the arrangement frequently, or opt for dried flowers, artificial blooms, or decorative fillers like colored sand, marbles, or pebbles. Arrange them creatively inside the bottle to create a visually appealing and unique centerpiece.

And there you have it! Your DIY upcycled bottle vase or centerpiece is now complete. Feel free to experiment with different bottle shapes, colors, and decorative techniques to suit your personal style and preferences. These upcycled creations also make wonderful gifts for friends and loved ones, showcasing your creativity and commitment to sustainability.

Remember, upcycling is all about breathing new life into discarded items and transforming them into functional and stylish creations. By choosing to upcycle glass bottles, not only are you reducing waste but also creating one-of-a-kind pieces that reflect your personal style. So go ahead and embrace the beauty of upcycling by creating stunning bottle vases or centerpieces that will be admired for years to come!.

- Glass bottle wind chimes

This guide will provide you with detailed instructions to help you bring this creative and aesthetically pleasing project to life.

They not only add a touch of whimsy and charm but also create soothing sounds as they gently sway in the breeze. Upcycling glass bottles into wind chimes is a sustainable and innovative way to give these discarded items a new purpose while adding a personal and artistic touch to your home or garden.

To start this project, you will need the following materials:

1. Glass bottles: The beauty of this DIY project lies in the variety of glass bottles you can use. Empty wine bottles, soda bottles, or any decorative glass bottles can all be upcycled for this purpose. Make sure to clean and remove any labels or adhesives from the bottles before beginning.

2. String or fishing line: This will be used to hang the glass bottles and create the chimes. Choose a strong and durable material that can withstand outdoor conditions.

3. Beads, crystals, or charms: These decorative elements will be attached to the string or fishing line between the glass bottles to add visual interest and enhance the overall aesthetics of the wind chimes. Select colors and designs that resonate with your personal style.

4. Drill or glass cutter: This is necessary if you plan to customize the glass bottles by drilling or cutting holes into them. It is recommended to use a drill or glass cutter specifically designed for glass to ensure a clean and safe process.

1. Clean and prepare the glass bottles: Before beginning any upcycling project, it is crucial to thoroughly clean and sanitize the glass bottles. Remove any labels, adhesive residues, or dirt from the surface. Make sure the bottles are completely dry before proceeding.

2. Design and customize the bottles: This step is optional but provides an opportunity to add a unique touch to your wind chimes. Using a drill or glass cutter, create holes in the bottom of the glass bottles. You can also experiment with drilling or cutting designs into the sides of the bottles to allow light to pass through. Be creative and let your imagination guide you.

3. String the glass bottles: Take the string or fishing line and cut it into lengths suitable for your desired chime length. Pass the string through the holes or around the neck of the bottle and tie secure knots to hold them in place. Leave a sufficient length

of string at the top for attaching the wind chime to a hook or hanger.

4. Add decorative elements: Enhance the visual appeal of your wind chimes by stringing beads, crystals, or charms between the glass bottles. This will add movement, sparkle, and a personal touch to your creation. Space them out evenly along the strings to create a balanced and visually pleasing composition.

5. Hang and enjoy: Once you have completed stringing the glass bottles and adding decorative elements, find a suitable outdoor location to hang your wind chimes. You can hang them from a tree branch, a porch, or even a shepherd's hook specifically designed for wind chimes. Ensure they are hung securely to withstand wind conditions.

As your wind chimes sway and produce gentle sounds, take a moment to appreciate the magic you have created by repurposing glass bottles into something beautiful and functional. The interplay of light, color, and sound will create a serene and inviting ambiance in your outdoor space.

Have fun exploring different bottle shapes, colors, and designs to create a unique and captivating sound experience.

Chapter 19: Repurposing Tin Cans

- Tin can planters

In this chapter, we will explore the exciting world of repurposing tin cans to create unique and stylish planters for your home. Transforming everyday items into functional and aesthetically pleasing creations is a fulfilling artistic endeavor that allows us to reduce waste and showcase our creativity.

To begin, gather your materials. You will need tin cans of various sizes, a hammer and nail, a ruler, a pencil, potting soil, and the plant of your choice. It's important to have a variety of sizes to create a visually appealing composition.

Start by preparing your tin cans. Make sure they are clean and free from any labels or adhesive residue. You can use warm soapy water to clean them thoroughly. Once they are dry, select the cans you wish to repurpose and remove the lids with a can opener.

Next, it's time to punch drainage holes in the bottom of each tin can. This step is crucial to ensure proper water drainage for your plants. Place the can on a sturdy surface, such as a wooden block, and use a hammer and nail to create several small holes. Space them evenly across the bottom of the can, ensuring they are not too close to the edges to maintain the structural integrity of the can.

Decorate the exterior of the cans using various techniques, such as painting, decoupage, or wrapping them in fabric or twine. Let your creativity shine and create unique designs that suit your personal style and home decor.

Fill each can about two-thirds full, leaving enough space for the root ball of your chosen plant.

Gently tap the cans on a flat surface to settle the soil and provide stability for your plants.

Consider the size of the can and the light conditions in your chosen location. Carefully remove your plant from its original container and gently place it into the can, ensuring the base of the plant is level with the top edge of the can. Add more soil if needed and gently press it down to secure the plant in place.

Whether indoors or outdoors, they will add a vibrant touch to any space. Ensure they receive adequate sunlight or shade depending on the plant's requirements and water them regularly, allowing the excess water to drain through the holes in the bottom.

By repurposing tin cans into unique planters, you are not only reducing waste but also adding a touch of greenery to your surroundings. The possibilities are endless when it comes to transforming everyday items into functional and stylish creations.

Happy crafting!.

- DIY tin can lanterns

Tin cans, often found in abundance in most households, can be transformed into stunning decorative pieces that provide ambient lighting. Through this step-by-step guide, I will share with you my personal DIY project in creating tin can lanterns that are sure to enhance the aesthetic appeal of your home.

To begin this project, gather the following materials:

- Tin cans (varying sizes and shapes).

- Hammer and nail.

- Gloves (preferably thick and protective).

- Pliers.

- Heat-resistant spray paint.

- Tea light candles or battery-operated LED lights.

- Wire or twine for hanging.

- Decorative materials (optional).

Firstly, ensure that you have collected an assortment of tin cans in varying sizes and shapes. Cleaning the can thoroughly is vital to achieve desirable results. Remove any labels, wash the cans with soap and warm water, and make sure they are completely dry before proceeding.

For safety purposes, it is advisable to wear gloves during the next steps to avoid any mishaps. Take a tin can and hold it firmly with a pair of pliers. Using a hammer and nail, make a series of holes around the bottom perimeter of the can, leaving about half an inch of space between each hole. This will allow for proper air circulation and the release of light from within the can.

Once you have created the desired pattern of holes, proceed with adding a personal touch by spray-painting the outside of the tin cans with heat-resistant paint. This not only enhances the aesthetics but also protects the cans against rust and other environmental factors. Remember to follow the instructions provided by the paint manufacturer and apply multiple coats if necessary, ensuring each coat is allowed to dry fully before proceeding.

Once the paint has dried completely, place a tea light candle or battery-operated LED light inside the tin can. The choice of lighting option depends on personal preference and safety considerations. Tea light candles can provide a warm and cozy ambiance, while battery-operated LED lights offer convenience and eliminate the risk of fire hazards.

To hang your tin can lanterns, securely attach a wire or twine to the top edge of each can. This will serve as the hanger. Be creative and experiment with different lengths to achieve an aesthetically pleasing display. Alternatively, you can place the lanterns on a flat surface to create an enchanting centerpiece or along a walkway for a mesmerizing glow.

If desired, you can further accessorize your tin can lanterns with decorative materials such as ribbons, beads, or other small trinkets. This allows for customization to match your personal style or themed events and special occasions.

Remember, the beauty of repurposing is that it promotes sustainability and gives new life to objects that would otherwise be discarded. By transforming ordinary tin cans into exquisite lanterns, you not only reduce waste but also create stunning décor pieces.

As you embark on this DIY project, make sure to exercise caution and prioritize safety. Always handle tools with care, especially when dealing with sharp objects such as nails or cans. In addition, ensure proper disposal of any waste materials according to local regulations.

Get creative, experiment with different patterns and colors, and have fun repurposing these everyday items into functional and stylish creations. Enjoy the process and the beautiful ambience these lanterns will bring to your home!.

- Tin can pencil holder

This guide will help you utilize tin cans to create a practical and aesthetically pleasing addition to your workspace.

Before we dive into the process, let's briefly discuss the concept of repurposing and upcycling. Repurposing is the act of finding new uses for old and discarded items, while upcycling involves transforming these items into something more valuable and functional. By repurposing tin cans, we can reduce waste and add a touch of creativity to our everyday lives.

- Tin cans (empty and cleaned).
- Acrylic paint in your preferred colors.
- Paintbrushes.
- Clear varnish or sealer.
- Sandpaper.

1. Prepare the tin cans: Begin by removing any labels or stickers from the tin cans. Wash them thoroughly with soap and warm water to ensure they are clean. If any sharp edges are present, carefully sand them down with sandpaper. Lastly, dry the tin cans completely before moving on to the next step.

2. It can be a pattern, a simple color block, or even a custom illustration! Let your creative instincts guide you in this step.

3. Paint the tin cans: Take your paintbrushes and start applying the acrylic paint to the tin cans, following your chosen design. Remember to paint a base coat before applying any intricate details or additional layers of color. Allow each layer to dry before adding the next. To achieve an even finish, you may need to apply multiple coats of paint. Be patient and let the paint dry completely between layers.

4. Add finishing touches: Once you're satisfied with the painted design, let the paint dry completely,

and consider sealing it with a clear varnish or sealer. This step will not only protect the paint but also give your pencil holder a glossy and professional look.

5. Enjoy the practicality and visual appeal of your new creation!.

Although this guide focuses on tin cans, you can also explore repurposing options for plastic shower curtains, plastic laundry detergent bottles, plastic shampoo bottles, plastic lotion bottles, paper towel rolls, toilet paper rolls, plastic grocery bags, plastic food packaging, plastic clamshell containers, plastic takeout containers, plastic egg cartons, plastic milk jugs, plastic soda bottles, wine corks, wine bottles, glass jars, glass bottles, aluminum cans, and even paper bags. These items can be transformed into beautiful and functional creations when given a second life.

Let your imagination run wild and explore the magic of repurposing everyday items into functional and stylish creations. Happy crafting!.

Chapter 20: Upcycling Aluminum Cans

- Creating a soda can herb garden

This unique DIY project not only allows you to repurpose a commonly discarded item but also provides you with a functional and stylish addition to your home or garden.

To get started, gather some aluminum cans that you have on hand or that you can collect. Rinse them out thoroughly and allow them to dry completely. This step is important to ensure that there are no residual substances or odors left in the cans.

Next, carefully remove the top portion of the aluminum cans using a can opener or a pair of scissors. Be cautious while doing this to avoid any sharp edges. Once the top portion is removed, you will have a small planter-like container.

Once you have prepared the cans, it's time to turn them into suitable herb planters. Start by creating drainage holes in the bottom of each can. This will help prevent water from accumulating and causing root rot. Use a nail or a small drill to puncture a few holes in the bottom of each can.

Now, it's time to add soil to the cans. Choose a high-quality potting mix that is suitable for growing herbs. Fill each can with soil, leaving some space at the top to avoid overwatering.

Select the herbs that you would like to grow in your soda can herb garden. Popular choices include basil, parsley, thyme, and mint. Make sure to choose herbs that have similar light and water requirements, as this will make maintenance easier.

Carefully transplant the herbs into the prepared cans. Gently remove each herb from its original pot and place it in the can, making sure that the roots are covered with soil. Press the soil gently to secure the herb in place.

Find a suitable location for your soda can herb garden. Herbs generally require at least 6-8 hours of sunlight each day, so pick a spot that receives ample sunshine. Consider placing your herb garden near a window, on a balcony, or in a garden bed.

Water your herbs regularly but avoid overwatering. Allow the soil to dry out slightly between waterings. You can monitor the moisture level by sticking your finger about an inch into the soil - if it feels dry, it's time to water.

As your herbs grow, you can harvest them for use in cooking or for various other purposes. Trim the plants regularly to encourage bushier growth. Enjoy the fragrance and flavors of your freshly grown herbs as you incorporate them into your culinary creations.

By following the steps outlined in this guide, you can successfully transform these everyday items into a beautiful herb garden that provides fresh ingredients for your culinary endeavors.

- DIY aluminum can coasters

As a skilled artisan in the world of DIY productions, I am delighted to guide you through the process of transforming aluminum cans into functional and stylish additions to your home decor.

To get started, gather the following materials:

1. Clean aluminum cans: Make sure to thoroughly wash the cans to remove any residue or labels. Allow them to dry completely before proceeding with the project.

2. Utility knife or sharp scissors: These tools will come in handy when cutting the aluminum cans into coaster-sized pieces.

3. Sandpaper: Use fine-grit sandpaper to smooth the edges of the cut aluminum cans, ensuring a safe and polished finish.

4. Protective gloves: It's important to wear gloves while working with sharp tools and materials to prevent any injuries.

5. Craft glue or clear adhesive: This will be used to attach a protective backing to the bottom of the coaster, preventing any scratches on surfaces.

Step 1: Prepare the aluminum cans.

Using your utility knife or sharp scissors, carefully cut off the top and bottom of the aluminum can. Make a vertical slit from the top to the bottom of the can and then cut along the outer edge of the can to remove the cylindrical section. Be cautious while cutting and hold the can firmly to prevent any accidents.

Step 2: Cut the aluminum can into coaster-sized circles.

Measure and mark the desired size of your coasters on the aluminum can sheets. Using your utility knife or sharp scissors, carefully cut out circular pieces from the can sheets. Take your time during this step to ensure clean and precise cuts.

Step 3: Smooth the edges.

Using fine-grit sandpaper, gently sand the edges of the aluminum can coasters to remove any sharpness or rough edges. This step will enhance the safety, durability, and overall finished look of your coasters. Be sure to wipe away any residue after sanding.

Step 4: Apply a protective backing.

To prevent any scratches on surfaces, attached a protective backing to the bottom of each coaster. Craft glue or a clear adhesive works well for this purpose. Apply a thin layer of adhesive onto the backing material (such as felt or cork) and firmly press it onto the bottom of the coaster. Allow the adhesive to dry completely as per the manufacturer's instructions.

Step 5: Finishing touches.

Ensure that all the edges are smooth and that the backing is securely attached. Wipe the coasters clean before placing them on any surface.

Congratulations! You have successfully transformed aluminum cans into stylish and functional DIY coasters. These unique creations not only repurpose materials that would otherwise go to waste but also add a touch of creativity and sustainability to your home decor. Enjoy your new coasters and continue exploring the world of upcycling and repurposing everyday items!.

- Aluminum can flower ornaments

This guide will provide you with a detailed step-by-step process to create these stunning decorations.

To begin this project, gather the following materials: aluminum cans (preferably for soda or beer), a pair of scissors or tin snips, a marker or pencil, sandpaper, wire cutters, floral wire or pipe cleaners, small beads or decorative pieces, and a hot glue gun.

Start by preparing your aluminum cans. Using the marker or pencil, draw various flower shapes onto the surface of the cans. You can create a variety of sizes and shapes to add visual interest to your ornaments. Once you have outlined the shapes, carefully cut them out using the scissors or tin snips. Take caution as the edges of the cans can be sharp, consider wearing gloves for added safety.

Next, take the cut-out aluminum flower shapes and gently sand the edges to smooth out any rough edges or sharp points. This step will also help remove any printed label or residue on the surface of the can.

Now it's time to give your aluminum flower ornaments some dimension. Using the wire cutters, snip a piece of floral wire or pipe cleaner to your desired length for each flower. Make sure to cut enough wire to form a stem and allow for attachment to other flowers in your final arrangement.

Take one end of the wire and fold it over about an inch to create a loop. This loop will secure the wire to the flower shape. Holding the folded end of the wire against the backside of the aluminum flower, carefully hot glue it in place. Press firmly to ensure a strong bond.

Once the glue has dried, you can add an extra touch of creativity to your aluminum flower ornaments by attaching small beads or other decorative pieces. Simply apply a small dot of hot glue onto the flower shape and press the desired embellishment onto it. Allow the glue to cool and set before handling.

Repeat these steps for each aluminum flower ornament you wish to create. Once you have a collection of flowers, feel free to experiment with different color combinations by using various colors of spray paint designed for metal surfaces. Remember to apply the spray paint in a well-ventilated area and follow the manufacturer's instructions for best results.

Allow the paint to fully dry before arranging your aluminum flower ornaments in a vase or other decorative display. You can mix and match different shapes, sizes, and colors to create a vibrant and whimsical arrangement.

With a bit of creativity and some simple materials, you can transform everyday aluminum cans into beautiful, eye-catching decorations that deserve a place in your living space.

Chapter 21: Repurposing Paper Bags

- Creating gift wrap or gift bags

Not only does it help reduce waste, but it also allows you to add a personal and unique touch to your gifts. In this chapter, we will explore the creative ways in which you can transform paper bags into stylish and functional gift wrap or gift bags.

To start off, gather all the paper bags you have on hand. Ideally, choose bags that are in good condition, without tears or stains. If you don't have any paper bags readily available, you can always ask for extras at your local grocery store or repurpose paper shopping bags from your previous purchases. Remember, the more colorful and patterned the bags are, the more visually interesting your gift wrap or gift bags will be.

Start by flattening the paper bags and smoothing out any creases or wrinkles. This will ensure a clean and polished finished product. Once flattened, you can decide whether you want to maintain the original size of the bag or resize it to fit your specific gift. If resizing is necessary, use a ruler and scissors to trim the bag accordingly.

Next, let your creativity shine by customizing the paper bag. There are several ways you can do this. Let's explore a few options:

1. Custom Stamps: Create your own stamps using objects from around the house, such as potato halves, sponges, or even carved erasers. Use acrylic or fabric paint to apply the design onto the paper bag. This technique allows you to create unique patterns or images on the bag.

2. Hand-Painted Designs: If you enjoy painting, this is the perfect opportunity to showcase your artistic skills. Use waterproof or acrylic paint to create beautiful motifs or illustrations directly onto

the paper bag. You can even experiment with different painting techniques like watercolor or stenciling.

3. Collage: Gather colorful magazine cutouts, decorative papers, or even fabric scraps to create a collage effect on the paper bag. Use glue or double-sided tape to attach the materials onto the bag, layering them for added visual interest.

4. Natural Elements: If you prefer a more rustic or organic look, consider incorporating natural elements like twigs, leaves, or flowers onto the paper bag. Secure them in place with glue or twine for an earthy and bohemian vibe.

Once you have personalized your paper bag, it's time to assemble it into a gift wrap or gift bag. If you want to create a gift wrap, simply fold the paper bag along the existing creases and use tape or glue to secure the edges. You can also add a decorative ribbon or twine for a finishing touch.

To transform the paper bag into a gift bag, begin by folding the bag where the sides meet the bottom. Fold the bottom end upwards to create a base for the bag. Use glue or staples to secure the sides in place. Finally, punch holes near the top of the bag and thread a ribbon through them to create handles.

Now that you have successfully repurposed a paper bag into a stylish gift wrap or gift bag, it's time to impress your recipients with your eco-friendly and creative approach to gifting. Remember, the possibilities are endless when it comes to repurposing everyday items. So, continue exploring and innovating, and transform your DIY creations into functional and stylish masterpieces.

- DIY paper bag lanterns

By upcycling ordinary paper bags, you can transform them into stylish and unique lighting fixtures that add a touch of charm and warmth to any space. Get ready to embark on a fun and creative project that not only benefits the environment but also adds a personal touch to your home decor.

To begin, gather the following materials:

- Paper bags (in any size and color you prefer).

- Craft knife or scissors.

- Hole puncher.

- Glue or adhesive tape.

- LED candles or battery-operated tea lights.

1. Choose the paper bags: Select paper bags that are sturdy and in good condition. You can reuse paper shopping bags or even plain brown lunch bags. Feel free to experiment with different sizes and colors to suit your aesthetic preferences.

2. Design your patterns: Decide on the design or pattern that you would like to create on your paper bag lantern. This can be a simple design, such as stars or hearts, or you can get creative and draw intricate patterns. The possibilities are endless!.

3. Cut out the design: Using a craft knife or scissors, carefully cut out your chosen design from the paper bag. Take your time and be mindful of the details. Remember to leave some space around the edges of the design to ensure the structural integrity of the bag.

4. Punch holes for ventilation and light: To allow proper ventilation and to create a beautiful light pattern, use a hole puncher to create small holes in the areas surrounding your design. These holes will allow light to shine through and create a mesmerizing effect.

5. Assembly: Once you have cut out your design and punched the necessary holes, it's time to assemble your DIY paper bag lantern. Apply glue or adhesive tape along the edges and fold the bag in a way that forms a cylinder. Press firmly to secure the edges together.

6. Illuminate your lantern: Place an LED candle or a battery-operated tea light inside the DIY paper bag lantern. The soft flickering light will cast

enchanting shadows through the cut-out patterns, creating a cozy and romantic ambiance in any room.

7. Display and enjoy: Find the perfect spot to display your DIY paper bag lantern. Hang them from the ceiling using strings or hooks, place them on shelves, or use them as centerpieces for special occasions. You can even create a cluster of lanterns in different sizes and patterns to add visual interest.

Remember to never use real candles or open flames inside the paper bag lanterns as they can be a fire hazard. LED candles or battery-operated tea lights are a safe alternative that still creates a beautiful ambiance.

By repurposing paper bags into DIY lanterns, you not only give these everyday items a new lease of life but also contribute to sustainable living. Upcycling and repurposing allow us to reduce waste and add unique touches to our living spaces.

.

- Paper bag scrapbook album

This unique project is not only a great way to repurpose materials, but also allows for endless creativity and personalization. In this chapter, we will focus on repurposing paper bags to create the pages of your scrapbook album.

To start, gather your materials. You will need paper bags, scissors, a ruler, a hole punch, decorative materials such as stamps or stickers, and adhesive or glue.

Begin by selecting paper bags of your choice. You can use different sizes and colors to add visual interest to your album. Lay the paper bag flat on your work surface and carefully cut off the bottom and remove any handles. This will give you a single sheet of paper from each bag.

Next, determine the size you want your album pages to be. Measure and mark the desired dimensions on the paper bag sheet, ensuring they are consistent across all pages. Use the ruler to draw straight lines connecting the marks, creating rectangular pages.

Once you have all your pages cut and prepared, it's time to add some charm and personality to them. This is where your creativity shines. You can use a variety of techniques such as stamping, stenciling, or even hand-drawn illustrations to decorate the pages. Think about the theme or purpose of your album and choose designs and colors that align with it. If you prefer a more minimalist look, you can also opt for elegant stickers or embossed details.

After decorating the pages, it's time to assemble the album. Stack your pages together, aligning the holes on the left side. Use a hole punch to create evenly spaced holes along the side of the pages. This will allow you to bind them together using ribbons, string, or even metal binder rings.

Once you have the binding holes punched, you can customize the cover of your album. You can use a larger paper bag to create a sturdy cover or use a different material like cardboard or chipboard.

Decorate the cover to your liking, keeping in mind that it will be the first thing people see when they come across your scrapbook album.

Finally, thread your chosen binding material through the holes in your album pages, securing them together. Tie a knot or a bow at the top or bottom to keep everything in place.

Congratulations, you have successfully repurposed paper bags to create a unique and personalized scrapbook album! This album will not only showcase your creativity and craftsmanship but also serve as a beautiful keepsake for your memories.

Remember, the possibilities are endless when it comes to DIY projects. By repurposing everyday items such as plastic shower curtains, laundry detergent bottles, shampoo bottles, and more, you can create functional and stylish creations. Happy crafting!.

Printed in Great Britain
by Amazon